Pennsylvania Constitution

The United States Constitution

The Declaration of Independence

and other facts about the
"Keystone State"

by
Annette C. Baker

To William Penn, a man who did not get to see all of the generations who have lived in freedom because of his work and sacrifice.

"Men must be governed by God, or they will be ruled by tyrants." - William Penn

"There can be no Friendship where there is no Freedom." - William Penn

Table of Contents

CONSTITUTION of the COMMONWEALTH OF PENNSYLVANIA

ARTICLE II. THE LEGISLATURE 28

ARTICLE IV. THE EXECUTIVE 49

ARTICLE V. THE JUDICIARY 59

SCHEDULES TO
CONSTITUTION OF PENNSYLVANIA 137

THE UNITED STATES CONSTITUTION

CONSTITUTION of the COMMONWEALTH OF PENNSYLVANIA[1]

PREAMBLE

WE, the people of the Commonwealth of Pennsylvania, grateful to Almighty God for the blessings of civil and religious liberty, and humbly invoking His guidance, do ordain and establish this Constitution.

ARTICLE I
DECLARATION OF RIGHTS [2]

That the general, great and essential principles of liberty and free government may be recognized and unalterably established, WE DECLARE THAT--

SECTION
1. Inherent rights of mankind.
2. Political powers.
3. Religious freedom.
4. Religion.
5. Elections.
6. Trial by jury.
7. Freedom of press and speech; libels.
8. Security from searches and seizures.

SECTION 1. INHERENT RIGHTS OF MANKIND.

All men are born equally free and independent, and have certain inherent and indefeasible rights, among which are those of enjoying and defending life and liberty, of acquiring, possessing and protecting property and reputation, and of pursuing their own happiness.

SECTION 2. POLITICAL POWERS.

All power is inherent in the people, and all free governments are founded on their authority and instituted for their peace, safety and happiness. For the advancement of these ends they have at all times an inalienable and indefeasible right to alter, reform or abolish their government in such manner as they may think proper.

SECTION 3. RELIGIOUS FREEDOM.
All men have a natural and indefeasible right to worship Almighty God according to the dictates of their own consciences; no man can of right be compelled to attend, erect or support any place of worship, or to maintain any ministry against his consent; no human authority can, in any case whatever, control or interfere with the rights of conscience, and no preference shall ever be given by law to any religious establishments or modes of worship.

SECTION 4. RELIGION.
No person who acknowledges the being of a God and a future state of rewards and punishments shall, on account of his religious sentiments, be disqualified to hold any office or place of trust or profit under this Commonwealth.

SECTION 5. ELECTIONS.
Elections shall be free and equal; and no power, civil or military, shall at any time interfere to prevent the free exercise of the right of suffrage.

SECTION 6. TRIAL BY JURY. [3]
Trial by jury shall be as heretofore, and the right thereof remain inviolate. The General Assembly may provide, however, by law, that a verdict may be rendered by not less than five-sixths of the jury in

any civil case. Furthermore, in criminal cases the Commonwealth shall have the same right to trial by jury as does the accused.

SECTION 7. FREEDOM OF PRESS AND SPEECH; LIBELS. [4]

The printing press shall be free to every person who may undertake to examine the proceedings of the Legislature or any branch of government, and no law shall ever be made to restrain the right thereof. The free communication of thoughts and opinions is one of the invaluable rights of man, and every citizen may freely speak, write and print on any subject, being responsible for the abuse of that liberty. No conviction shall be had in any prosecution for the publication of papers relating to the official conduct of officers or men in public capacity, or to any other matter proper for public investigation or information, where the fact that such publication was not maliciously or negligently made shall be established to the satisfaction of the jury; and in all indictments for libels the jury shall have the right to determine the law and the facts, under the direction of the court, as in other cases.

SECTION 8. SECURITY FROM SEARCHES AND SEIZURES.

The people shall be secure in their persons, houses, papers and possessions from unreasonable searches and seizures, and no warrant to search any place or to seize any person or things shall issue without describing them as nearly as may be, nor without probable cause, supported by oath or affirmation subscribed to by the affiant.

SECTION 9. RIGHTS OF ACCUSED IN CRIMINAL PROSECUTIONS. [5]

In all criminal prosecutions the accused hath a right to be heard by himself and his counsel, to demand the nature and cause of the accusation against him, to be confronted with the witnesses against him, to have compulsory process for obtaining witnesses in his favor, and, in prosecutions by indictment or information, a speedy public trial by an impartial jury of the vicinage; he cannot be compelled to give evidence against himself, nor can he be deprived of his life, liberty or property, unless by the judgment of his peers or the law of the land. The use of a suppressed voluntary admission or voluntary confession to impeach the credibility of a person may be permitted and shall not be construed as compelling a person to give evidence against himself.

SECTION 10. INITIATION OF CRIMINAL PROCEEDINGS; TWICE IN JEOPARDY; EMINENT DOMAIN. [6]

Except as hereinafter provided no person shall, for any indictable offense, be proceeded against criminally by information, except in cases arising in the land or naval forces, or in the militia, when in actual service, in time of war or public danger, or by leave of the court for oppression or misdemeanor in office. Each of the several courts of common pleas may, with the approval of the Supreme Court, provide for the initiation of criminal proceedings therein by information filed in the manner provided by law. No person shall, for the same offense, be twice put in jeopardy of life or limb; nor shall private property be taken or applied to public use, without authority of law and without just compensation being first made or secured.

SECTION 11. COURTS TO BE OPEN; SUITS AGAINST THE COMMONWEALTH.

All courts shall be open; and every man for an injury done him in his lands, goods, person or reputation shall have remedy by due course of law, and right and justice administered without sale, denial or delay. Suits may be brought against the Commonwealth in such manner, in such courts and in such cases as the Legislature may by law direct.

SECTION 12. POWER OF SUSPENDING LAWS.

No power of suspending laws shall be exercised unless by the Legislature or by its authority.

SECTION 13. BAIL, FINES AND PUNISHMENTS.

Excessive bail shall not be required, nor excessive fines imposed, nor cruel punishments inflicted.

SECTION 14. PRISONERS TO BE BAILABLE; HABEAS CORPUS. [7]

All prisoners shall be bailable by sufficient sureties, unless for capital offenses or for offenses for which the maximum sentence is life imprisonment or unless no condition or combination of conditions other than imprisonment will reasonably assure the safety of any person and the community when the proof is evident or presumption great; and the privilege of the writ of habeas corpus shall not be suspended, unless when in case of rebellion or invasion the public safety may require it.

SECTION 15. SPECIAL CRIMINAL TRIBUNALS. [8]

No commission shall issue creating special temporary criminal tribunals to try particular individuals or particular classes of cases.

SECTION 16. INSOLVENT DEBTORS.

The person of a debtor, where there is not strong presumption of fraud, shall not be continued in prison after delivering up his estate for the benefit of his creditors in such manner as shall be prescribed by law.

SECTION 17. EX POST FACTO LAWS;
IMPAIRMENT OF CONTRACTS.

No ex post facto law, nor any law impairing the obligation of contracts, or making irrevocable any grant of special privileges or immunities, shall be passed.

SECTION 18. ATTAINDER.

No person shall be attainted of treason or felony by the Legislature.

SECTION 19. ATTAINDER LIMITED. [9]

No attainder shall work corruption of blood, nor, except during the life of the offender, forfeiture of estate to the Commonwealth.

SECTION 20. RIGHT OF PETITION.

The citizens have a right in a peaceable manner to assemble together for their common good, and to apply to those invested with the powers of government for redress of grievances or other proper purposes, by petition, address or remonstrance

SECTION 21. RIGHT TO BEAR ARMS.

The right of the citizens to bear arms in defense of themselves and the State shall not be questioned.

SECTION 22. STANDING ARMY; MILITARY SUBORDINATE TO CIVIL POWER.

No standing army shall, in time of peace, be kept up without the consent of the Legislature, and the military shall in all cases and at all times be in strict subordination to the civil power.

SECTION 23. QUARTERING OF TROOPS.

No soldier shall in time of peace be quartered in any house without the consent of the owner, nor in time of war but in a manner to be prescribed by law.

SECTION 24. TITLES AND OFFICES.

The Legislature shall not grant any title of nobility or hereditary distinction, nor create any office the appointment to which shall be for a longer term than during good behavior.

SECTION 25. RESERVATION OF POWERS IN PEOPLE. [10]

To guard against transgressions of the high powers which we have delegated, we declare that everything in this article is excepted out of the general powers of government and shall forever remain inviolate.

SECTION 26. NO DISCRIMINATION BY COMMONWEALTH AND ITS POLITICAL SUBDIVISIONS. [11]

Neither the Commonwealth nor any political subdivision thereof shall deny to any person the enjoyment of any civil right, nor discriminate against any person in the exercise of any civil right.

SECTION 27. NATURAL RESOURCES AND THE PUBLIC ESTATE. [12]

The people have a right to clean air, pure water, and to the preservation of the natural, scenic, historic and esthetic values of the environment. Pennsylvania's public natural resources are the common property of all the people, including generations yet to come. As trustee of these resources, the Commonwealth shall conserve and maintain them for the benefit of all the people.

SECTION 28. PROHIBITION AGAINST DENIAL OR ABRIDGMENT OF EQUALITY OF RIGHTS BECAUSE OF SEX. [13]

Equality of rights under the law shall not be denied or abridged in the Commonwealth of Pennsylvania because of the sex of the individual.

ARTICLE II
THE LEGISLATURE [14]

SECTION 1. LEGISLATIVE POWER.

The legislative power of this Commonwealth shall be vested in a General Assembly, which shall consist of a Senate and a House of Representatives.

SECTION 2. ELECTION OF MEMBERS; VACANCIES.

Members of the General Assembly shall be chosen at the general election every second year. Their term of service shall begin on the first (1st) day of December next after their election. Whenever a vacancy shall occur in either House, the presiding officer thereof shall issue a writ of election to fill such vacancy for the remainder of the term.

28

SECTION 3. TERMS OF MEMBERS.

Senators shall be elected for the term of four (4) years and Representatives for the term of two (2) years.

SECTION 4. SESSIONS. [15]

The General Assembly shall be a continuing body during the term for which its Representatives are elected. It shall meet at 12 o'clock noon on the first Tuesday of January each year. Special sessions shall be called by the Governor on petition of a majority of the members elected to each House or may be called by the Governor whenever in his opinion the public interest requires.

SECTION 5. QUALIFICATIONS OF MEMBERS.

Senators shall be at least twenty five (25) years of age and Representatives twenty one (21) years of age. They shall have been citizens and inhabitants of the State four years, and inhabitants of their respective districts one year next before their election (unless absent on the public business of the United States or of this State), and shall reside in their respective districts during their terms of service.

SECTION 6. DISQUALIFICATION TO HOLD OTHER OFFICE. [16]

No Senator or Representative shall, during the time for which he was elected, be appointed to any civil office under this Commonwealth to which a salary, fee or perquisite is attached. No member of Congress or other person holding any office (except of attorney-at-law or in the National Guard or in a reserve component of the armed forces of the United

States) under the United States or this Commonwealth to which a salary, fee or perquisite is attached shall be a member of either House during his continuance in office.

SECTION 7. INELIGIBILITY BY CRIMINAL CONVICTIONS.

No person hereafter convicted of embezzlement of public moneys, bribery, perjury or other infamous crime, shall be eligible to the General Assembly, or capable of holding any office of trust or profit in this Commonwealth.

SECTION 8. COMPENSATION.

The members of the General Assembly shall receive such salary and mileage for regular and special sessions as shall be fixed by law, and no other compensation whatever, whether for service upon committee or otherwise. No member of either House shall during the term for which he may have been elected, receive any increase of salary, or mileage, under any law passed during such term.

SECTION 9. ELECTION OF OFFICERS; JUDGE OF ELECTION AND QUALIFICATIONS OF MEMBERS.

The Senate shall, at the beginning and close of each regular session and at such other times as may be necessary, elect one (1) of its members President pro tempore, who shall perform the duties of the Lieutenant Governor, in any case of absence or disability of that officer, and whenever the said office of Lieutenant Governor shall be vacant. The House of Representatives shall elect one (1) of its members as Speaker. Each House shall choose its other officers, and shall judge of the election and qualifications of its members.

SECTION 10. QUORUM.
A majority of each House shall constitute a quorum, but a smaller number may adjourn from day to day and compel the attendance of absent members.

SECTION 11. POWERS OF EACH HOUSE; EXPULSION.
Each House shall have power to determine the rules of its proceedings and punish its members or other persons for contempt or disorderly behavior in its presence, to enforce obedience to its process, to protect its members against violence or offers of bribes or private solicitation, and, with the concurrence of two-thirds (2/3), to expel a member, but not a second time for the same cause, and shall have all other powers necessary for the Legislature of a free State. A member expelled for corruption shall not thereafter be eligible to either House, and punishment for contempt or disorderly behavior shall not bar an indictment for the same offense.

SECTION 12. JOURNALS; YEAS AND NAYS.
Each House shall keep a journal of its proceedings and from time to time publish the same, except such parts as require secrecy, and the yeas and nays of the members on any question shall, at the desire of any two of them, be entered on the journal.

SECTION 13. OPEN SESSIONS.

The sessions of each House and of committees of the whole shall be open, unless when the business is such as ought to be kept secret.

SECTION 14. ADJOURNMENTS.

Neither House shall, without the consent of the other, adjourn for more than three (3) days, nor to any other place than that in which the two (2) Houses shall be sitting.

SECTION 15. PRIVILEGES OF MEMBERS.

The members of the General Assembly shall in all cases, except treason, felony, violation of their oath of office, and breach or surety of the peace, be privileged from arrest during their attendance at the sessions of their respective Houses and in going to and returning from the same; and for any speech or debate in either House they shall not be questioned in any other place.

SECTION 16. LEGISLATIVE DISTRICTS. [17]

The Commonwealth shall be divided into fifty (50) senatorial and two hundred three (203) representative districts, which shall be composed of compact and contiguous territory as nearly equal in population as practicable. Each senatorial district shall elect one Senator, and each representative district one Representative. Unless absolutely necessary no county, city, incorporated town, borough, township or ward shall be divided in forming either a senatorial or representative district.

SECTION 17. LEGISLATIVE REAPPORTIONMENT COMMISSION. [18]

(a) In each year following the year of the Federal decennial census, a Legislative Reapportionment Commission shall be constituted for the purpose of reapportioning the Commonwealth. The commission shall act by a majority of its entire membership.

(b) The commission shall consist of five members: four (4) of whom shall be the majority and minority leaders of both the Senate and the House of Representatives, or deputies appointed by each of them, and a chairman selected as hereinafter provided. No later than sixty (60) days following the official reporting of the Federal decennial census as required by Federal law, the four members shall be certified by the President *pro tempore* of the Senate and the Speaker of the House of Representatives to the elections officer of the Commonwealth who under law shall have supervision over elections. The four (4) members within forty-five (45) days after their certification shall select the fifth (5th) member, who shall serve as chairman of the commission, and shall immediately certify his name to such elections officer. The chairman shall be a citizen of the Commonwealth other than a local, State or Federal official holding an office to which compensation is attached. If the four (4) members fail to select the fifth (5th) member within the time prescribed, a majority of the entire membership of the Supreme Court within thirty (30) days thereafter shall appoint the chairman as aforesaid and certify his appointment to such elections officer. Any vacancy in the commission shall be filled within fifteen (15) days in the same manner in which such position was originally filled.

(c) No later than ninety (90) days after either the commission has been duly certified or the population data for the Commonwealth as determined by the

Federal decennial census are available, whichever is later in time, the commission shall file a preliminary reapportionment plan with such elections officer. The commission shall have thirty (30) days after filing the preliminary plan to make corrections in the plan. Any person aggrieved by the preliminary plan shall have the same thirty (30) day period to file exceptions with the commission in which case the commission shall have thirty (30) days after the date the exceptions were filed to prepare and file with such elections officer a revised reapportionment plan. If no exceptions are filed within thirty (30) days, or if filed and acted upon, the commissions's plan shall be final and have the force of law.

(d) Any aggrieved person may file an appeal from the final plan directly to the Supreme Court within thirty (30) days after the filing thereof. If the appellant establishes that the final plan is contrary to law, the Supreme Court shall issue an order remanding the plan to the commission and directing the commission to reapportion the Commonwealth in a manner not inconsistent with such order.

(e) When the Supreme Court has finally decided an appeal or when the last day for filing an appeal has passed with no appeal taken, the reapportionment plan shall have the force of law and the d stricts therein provided shall be used thereafter in elections to the General Assembly until the next reapportionment as required under this Section 17.

(f) Any district which does not include the res dence from which a member of the Senate was elected whether or not scheduled for election at the next general election shall elect a Senator at such election.

(g) The General Assembly shall appropriate sufficient funds for the compensation and expenses of members and staff appointed by the commission, and other necessary expenses. The members of the commission shall be entitled to such compensation for their services as the General Assembly from time to time shall determine, but no part thereof shall be paid until a preliminary plan is filed. If a preliminary plan is filed but the commission fails to file a revised or final plan within the time prescribed, the commission members shall forfeit all right to compensation not paid.

(h) If a preliminary, revised or final reapportionment plan is not filed by the commission within the time prescribed by this section, unless the time be extended by the Supreme Court for cause shown, the Supreme Court shall immediately proceed on its own motion to reapportion the Commonwealth.

(i) Any reapportionment plan filed by the commission, or ordered or prepared by the Supreme Court upon the failure of the commission to act, shall be published by the elections officer once in at least one newspaper of general circulation in each senatorial and representative district. The publication shall contain a map of the Commonwealth showing the complete reapportionment of the General Assembly by districts, and a map showing the reapportionment districts in the area normally served by the newspaper in which the publication is made. The publication shall also state the population of the senatorial and representative districts having the smallest and largest population and the percentage variation of such districts from the average population for senatorial and representative districts.

ARTICLE III
LEGISLATION[19]

A. PROCEDURE
SECTION
1. Passage of laws.
2. Reference to committee; printing.
3. Form of bills.
4. Consideration of bills.
5. Concurring in amendments; conference committee reports.
6. Revival and amendment of laws.
7. Notice of local and special bills.
8. Signing of bills.
9. Action on concurrent orders and resolutions.
10. Revenue bills.
11. Appropriation bills.
12. Legislation designated by Governor at special sessions.
13. Vote denied members with personal interest.

B. EDUCATION
SECTION
14. Public school system.
15. Public school money not available to sectarian schools.

C. NATIONAL GUARD
SECTION
16. National Guard to be organized and maintained.

D. OTHER LEGISLATION SPECIFICALLY AUTHORIZED
SECTION
17. Appointment of legislative officers and employees.
18. Compensation laws allowed to General Assembly.
19. Appropriations for support of widows and orphans of persons who served in the armed forces.
20. Classification of municipalities.
21. Land title registration.
22. State purchases.
23. Change of venue.
24. Paying out public moneys.

A. PROCEDURE
SECTION 1. PASSAGE OF LAWS.

No law shall be passed except by bill, and no bill shall be so altered or amended, on its passage through either House, as to change its original purpose.

SECTION 2. REFERENCE TO COMMITTEE; PRINTING.[20]

No bill shall be considered unless referred to a committee, printed for the use of the members and returned therefrom.

SECTION 3. FORM OF BILLS. [21]

No bill shall be passed containing more than one subject, which shall be clearly expressed in its title, except a general appropriation bill or a bill codifying or compiling the law or a part thereof.

SECTION 4. CONSIDERATION OF BILLS. [22]

Every bill shall be considered on three different days in each House. All amendments made thereto shall be printed for the use of the members before the final vote is taken on the bill and before the final vote is taken, upon written request addressed to the presiding officer of either House by at least 25% of the members elected to that House, any bill shall be read at length in that House. No bill shall become a law, unless on its final passage the vote is taken by yeas and nays, the names of the persons voting for and against it are entered on the journal, and a majority of the members elected to each House is recorded thereon as voting in its favor.

SECTION 5. CONCURRING IN AMENDMENTS; CONFERENCE COMMITTEE REPORTS.

No amendment to bills by one House shall be concurred in by the other, except by the vote of a majority of the members elected thereto, taken by yeas and nays, and the names of those voting for and against recorded upon the journal thereof; and reports of committees of conference shall be adopted in either House only by the vote of a majority of the members elected thereto, taken by yeas and nays, and the names of those voting recorded upon the journals.

SECTION 6. REVIVAL AND AMENDMENT OF LAWS.

No law shall be revived, amended, or the provisions thereof extended or conferred, by reference to its title only, but so much thereof as is revived, amended, extended or conferred shall be re-enacted and published at length.

SECTION 7. NOTICE OF LOCAL AND SPECIAL BILLS.[23]

No local or special bill shall be passed unless notice of the intention to apply therefor shall have been published in the locality where the matter or the thing to be effected may be situated, which notice shall be at least 30 days prior to the introduction into the General Assembly of such bill and in the manner to be provided by law; the evidence of such notice having been published, shall be exhibited in the General Assembly, before such act shall be passed.

SECTION 8. SIGNING OF BILLS. [24]

The presiding officer of each House shall, in the presence of the House over which he presides, sign all bills and joint resolutions passed by the General Assembly, after their titles have been publicly read immediately before signing; and the fact of signing shall be entered on the journal.

SECTION 9. ACTION ON CONCURRENT ORDERS AND RESOLUTIONS. [25]

Every order, resolution or vote, to which the concurrence of both Houses may be necessary, except on the question of adjournment, shall be presented to the Governor and before it shall take effect be approved by him, or being disapproved, shall be repassed by two-thirds (2/3) of both Houses according to the rules and limitations prescribed in case of a bill.

SECTION 10. REVENUE BILLS. [26]

All bills for raising revenue shall originate in the House of Representatives, but the Senate may propose amendments as in other bills.

SECTION 11. APPROPRIATION BILLS. [27]

The general appropriation bill shall embrace nothing but appropriations for the executive, legislative and judicial departments of the Commonwealth, for the public debt and for public schools. All other appropriations shall be made by separate bills, each embracing but one subject.

SECTION 12. LEGISLATION DESIGNATED BY GOVERNOR AT SPECIAL SESSIONS. [28]

When the General Assembly shall be convened in special session, there shall be no legislation upon subjects other than those designated in the proclamation of the Governor calling such session.

SECTION 13. VOTE DENIED MEMBERS WITH PERSONAL INTEREST. [29]

A member who has a personal or private interest in any measure or bill proposed or pending before the General Assembly shall disclose the fact to the House of which he is a member, and shall not vote thereon.

B. EDUCATION

SECTION 14. PUBLIC SCHOOL SYSTEM. [30]

The General Assembly shall provide for the maintenance and support of a thorough and efficient system of public education to serve the needs of the Commonwealth.

SECTION 15. PUBLIC SCHOOL MONEY NOT AVAILABLE TO SECTARIAN SCHOOLS. [31]

No money raised for the support of the public schools of the Commonwealth shall be appropriated to or used for the support of any sectarian school.

C. NATIONAL GUARD

SECTION 16. NATIONAL GUARD TO BE ORGANIZED AND MAINTAINED. [32]

The citizens of this Commonwealth shall be armed, organized and disciplined for its defense when and in such manner as may be directed by law. The General Assembly shall provide for maintaining the National Guard by appropriations from the Treasury of the Commonwealth, and may exempt from State military service persons having conscientious scruples against bearing arms.

D. OTHER LEGISLATION SPECIFICALLY AUTHORIZED[33]

SECTION 17. APPOINTMENT OF LEGISLATIVE OFFICERS AND EMPLOYEES.

The General Assembly shall prescribe by law the number, duties and compensation of the officers and employees of each House, and no payment shall be made from the State Treasury, or be in any way authorized, to any person, except to an acting officer or employee elected or appointed in pursuance of law.

SECTION 18. COMPENSATION LAWS ALLOWED TO GENERAL ASSEMBLY. [34]

The General Assembly may enact laws requiring the payment by employers, or employers and employees jointly, of reasonable compensation for injuries to employees arising in the course of their employment, and for occupational diseases of employees, whether or not such injuries or diseases result in death, and regardless of fault of employer or employee, and fixing the basis of ascertainment of such compensation and the maximum and minimum limits thereof, and providing special or general remedies for the collection thereof; but in no other cases shall the General Assembly limit the amount to be recovered for injuries resulting in death, or for injuries to persons or property, and in case of death from such injuries, the right of action shall survive, and the General Assembly shall prescribe for whose benefit such actions shall be prosecuted. No act shall prescribe any limitations of time within which suits may be brought against corporations for injuries to persons or property, or for other causes different from those fixed by general laws regulating actions against natural persons, and such acts now existing are avoided.

SECTION 19. APPROPRIATIONS FOR SUPPORT OF WIDOWS AND ORPHANS OF PERSONS WHO SERVED IN THE ARMED FORCES. [35]

The General Assembly may make appropriations of money to institutions wherein the widows of persons who served in the armed forces are supported or assisted, or the orphans of persons who served in the armed forces are maintained and educated; but such appropriations shall be applied exclusively to the support of such widows and orphans.

SECTION 20. CLASSIFICATION OF MUNICIPALITIES. [36]

The Legislature shall have power to classify counties, cities, boroughs, school districts, and townships according to population, and all laws passed relating to each class, and all laws passed relating to, and regulating procedure and proceedings in court with reference to, any class, shall be deemed general legislation within the meaning of this Constitution.

SECTION 21. LAND TITLE REGISTRATION. [37]

Laws may be passed providing for a system of registering, transferring, insuring of and guaranteeing land titles by the State, or by the counties thereof, and for settling and determining adverse or other claims to and interest in lands the titles to which are so registered, transferred, insured, and guaranteed; and for the creation and collection of indemnity funds; and for carrying the system and powers hereby provided for into effect by such existing courts as may be designated by the Legislature. Such laws may provide for continuing the registering, transferring, insuring, and guaranteeing such titles after the first or original registration has been perfected by the court, and provision may be made for raising the necessary funds for expenses and salaries of officers, which shall be paid out of the treasury of the several counties.

SECTION 22. STATE PURCHASES. [38]

The General Assembly shall maintain by law a system of competitive bidding under which all purchases of materials, printing, supplies or other personal property used by the government of this

Commonwealth shall so far as practicable be made. The law shall provide that no officer or employee of the Commonwealth shall be in any way interested in any purchase made by the Commonwealth under contract or otherwise.

SECTION 23. CHANGE OF VENUE.
The power to change the venue in civil and criminal cases shall be vested in the courts, to be exercised in such manner as shall be provided by law.

SECTION 24. PAYING OUT PUBLIC MONEYS. [39]
No money shall be paid out of the treasury, except on appropriations made by law and on warrant issued by the proper officers; but cash refunds of taxes, licenses, fees and other charges paid or collected, but not legally due, may be paid, as provided by law, without appropriation from the fund into which they were paid on warrant of the proper officer.

SECTION 25. EMERGENCY SEATS OF GOVERNMENT. [40]
The General Assembly may provide, by law, during any session, for the continuity of the executive, legislative, and judicial functions of the government of the Commonwealth, and its political subdivisions, and the establishment of emergency seats thereof and any such laws heretofore enacted are validated. Such legislation shall become effective in the event of an attack by an enemy of the United States.

SECTION 26. EXTRA COMPENSATION PROHIBITED; CLAIMS AGAINST THE COMMONWEALTH; PENSIONS. [41]

No bill shall be passed giving any extra compensation to any public officer, servant, employee, agent or contractor, after services shall have been rendered or contract made, nor providing for the payment of any claim against the Commonwealth without previous authority of law: Provided, however, That nothing in this Constitution shall be construed to prohibit the General Assembly from authorizing the increase of retirement allowances or pensions of members of a retirement or pension system now in effect or hereafter legally constituted by the Commonwealth, its political subdivisions, agencies or instrumentalities, after the termination of the services of said member.

SECTION 27. CHANGES IN TERM OF OFFICE OR SALARY PROHIBITED. [42]

No law shall extend the term of any public officer, or increase or diminish his salary or emoluments, after his election or appointment.

E. RESTRICTIONS ON LEGISLATIVE POWER

SECTION 28. CHANGE OF PERMANENT LOCATION OF STATE CAPITAL. [43]

No law changing the permanent location of the Capital of the State shall be valid until the same shall have been submitted to the qualified electors of the Commonwealth at a general election and ratified and approved by them.

SECTION 29. APPROPRIATIONS FOR PUBLIC ASSISTANCE, MILITARY SERVICE, SCHOLARSHIPS. [44]

No appropriation shall be made for charitable, educational or benevolent purposes to any person or community nor to any denominational and sectarian institution, corporation or association: Provided, That appropriations may be made for pensions or gratuities for military service and to blind persons 21 years of age and upwards and for assistance to mothers having dependent children and to aged persons without adequate means of support and in the form of scholarship grants or loans for higher educational purposes to residents of the Commonwealth enrolled in institutions of higher learning except that no scholarship, grants or loans for higher educational purposes shall be given to persons enrolled in a theological seminary or school of theology.

SECTION 30. CHARITABLE AND EDUCATIONAL APPROPRIATIONS. [45]

No appropriation shall be made to any charitable or educational institution not under the absolute control of the Commonwealth, other than normal schools established by law for the professional training of teachers for the public schools of the State, except by a vote of two-thirds (2/3) of all the members elected to each House.

SECTION 31. DELEGATION OF CERTAIN POWERS PROHIBITED.[46]

The General Assembly shall not delegate to any special commission, private corporation or association, any power to make, supervise or interfere with any municipal improvement, money, property or effects, whether held in trust or otherwise, or to levy taxes or perform any municipal function whatever. Notwithstanding the foregoing limitation or any other provision of the Constitution, the General Assembly may enact laws which provide that the findings of panels or commissions, selected and acting in accordance with law for the adjustment or settlement of grievances or disputes or for collective bargaining between policemen and firemen and their public employers shall be binding upon all parties and shall constitute a mandate to the head of the political subdivision which is the employer, or to the appropriate officer of the Commonwealth if the Commonwealth is the employer, with respect to matters which can be remedied by administrative action, and to the lawmaking body of such political subdivision or of the Commonwealth, with respect to matters which require legislative action, to take the action necessary to carry out such findings.

SECTION 32. CERTAIN LOCAL AND SPECIAL LAWS. [47]

The General Assembly shall pass no local or special law in any case which has been or can be provided for by general law and specifically the General Assembly shall not pass any local or special law:

1. Regulating the affairs of counties, cities, townships, wards, boroughs or school districts:
2. Vacating roads, town plats, streets or alleys:
3. Locating or changing county seats, erecting new counties or changing county lines:
4. Erecting new townships or boroughs, changing township lines, borough limits or school districts:

5. Remitting fines, penalties and forfeitures, or refunding moneys legally paid into the treasury:
6. Exempting property from taxation:
7. Regulating labor, trade, mining or manufacturing:
8. Creating corporations, or amending, renewing or extending the charters thereof:

Nor shall the General Assembly indirectly enact any special or local law by the partial repeal of a general law; but laws repealing local or special acts may be passed.

ARTICLE IV
THE EXECUTIVE [48]

SECTION 1. EXECUTIVE DEPARTMENT. [49]

The Executive Department of this Commonwealth shall consist of a Governor, Lieutenant Governor,

Attorney General, Auditor General, State Treasurer, and Superintendent of Public Instruction and such other officers as the General Assembly may from time to time prescribe.

SECTION 2. DUTIES OF GOVERNOR; ELECTION PROCEDURE; TIE OR CONTEST.

The supreme executive power shall be vested in the Governor, who shall take care that the laws be faithfully executed; he shall be chosen on the day of the general election, by the qualified electors of the Commonwealth, at the places where they shall vote for Representatives. The returns of every election for Governor shall be sealed up and transmitted to the seat of government, directed to the President of the Senate, who shall open and publish them in the presence of the members of both Houses of the General Assembly. The person having the highest number of votes shall be Governor, but if two or more be equal and highest in votes, one of them shall be chosen Governor by the joint vote of the members of both Houses. Contested elections shall be determined by a committee, to be selected from both Houses of the General Assembly, and formed and regulated in such manner as shall be directed by law.

SECTION 3. TERMS OF OFFICE OF GOVERNOR; NUMBER OF TERMS. [50]

The Governor shall hold his office during four years from the third (3rd) Tuesday of January next ensuing his election. Except for the Governor who may be in office when this amendment is adopted, he shall be eligible to succeed himself for one (1) additional term.

SECTION 4. LIEUTENANT GOVERNOR. [51]

A Lieutenant Governor shall be chosen jointly with the Governor by the casting by each voter of a single vote applicable to both offices, for the same term, and subject to the same provisions as the Governor; he shall be President of the Senate. As such, he may vote in case of a tie on any question except the final passage of a bill or joint resolution, the adoption of a conference report or the concurrence in amendments made by the House of Representatives.

SECTION 4.1. ATTORNEY GENERAL. [52]

An Attorney General shall be chosen by the qualified electors of the Commonwealth on the day the general election is held for the Auditor General and State Treasurer; he shall hold his office during four years from the third Tuesday of January next ensuing his election and shall not be eligible to serve continuously for more than two successive terms; he shall be the chief law officer of the Commonwealth and shall exercise such powers and perform such duties as may be imposed by law.

SECTION 5. QUALIFICATIONS OF GOVERNOR, LIEUTENANT GOVERNOR AND ATTORNEY GENERAL. [53]

No person shall be eligible to the office of Governor, Lieutenant Governor or Attorney General except a citizen of the United States, who shall have attained the age of 30 years, and have been seven (7) years next preceding his election an inhabitant of this Commonwealth, unless he shall have been absent on the public business of the United States or of this Commonwealth. No person shall be eligible to the office of Attorney General except a member of the bar of the Supreme Court of Pennsylvania.

SECTION 6. DISQUALIFICATION FOR OFFICES OF GOVERNOR, LIEUTENANT GOVERNOR AND ATTORNEY GENERAL [54]

No member of Congress or person holding any office (except of attorney-at-law or in the National Guard or in a reserve component of the armed forces of the United States) under the United States or this Commonwealth shall exercise the office of Governor, Lieutenant Governor or Attorney General.

SECTION 7. MILITARY POWER. [55]

The Governor shall be commander-in-chief of the military forces of the Commonwealth, except when they shall be called into actual service of the United States.

SECTION 8. APPOINTING POWER. [56]

(a) The Governor shall appoint a Secretary of Education and such other officers as he shall be authorized by law to appoint. The appointment of the Secretary of Education and of such other officers as may be specified by law, shall be subject to the consent of two-thirds or a majority of the members elected to the Senate as is specified by law.

(b) The Governor shall fill vacancies in offices to which he appoints by nominating to the Senate a proper person to fill the vacancy within 90 days of the first day of the vacancy and not thereafter. The Senate shall act on each executive nomination within 25 legislative days of its submission. If the Senate has not voted upon a nomination within 15 legislative days following such submission, any five members of the Senate may, in writing, request the presiding officer of the Senate to place the nomination before the entire Senate body whereby the nomination must be voted upon prior to the expiration of five legislative days or 25 legislative days following submission by the Governor, whichever occurs first. If the nomination is made during a recess or after adjournment *sine die*, the Senate shall act upon it within 25 legislative days after its return or reconvening. If the Senate for any reason fails to act upon a nomination submitted to it within the required 25 legislative days, the nominee shall take office as if the appointment had been consented to by the Senate. The Governor shall in a similar manner fill vacancies in the offices of Auditor General, State Treasurer, justice, judge, justice of the peace and in any other elective office he is authorized to fill. In the case of a vacancy in an elective office, a person shall be elected to the office on the next election day appropriate to the office unless the first day of the vacancy is within two calendar months immediately preceding the election day in which case the election shall be held on the second succeeding election day appropriate to the office.

(c) In acting on executive nominations, the Senate shall sit with open doors. The votes shall be taken by yeas and nays and shall be entered on the journal.

SECTION 9. PARDONING POWER; BOARD OF PARDONS. [57]

(a) In all criminal cases except impeachment the Governor shall have power to remit fines and forfeitures, to grant reprieves, commutation of sentences and pardons; but no pardon shall be granted, nor sentence commuted, except on the recommendation in writing of a majority of the Board of Pardons, and, in the case of a sentence of death or life imprisonment, on the unanimous recommendation in writing of the Board of Pardons, after full hearing in open session, upon due public notice. The recommendation, with the reasons therefor at length, shall be delivered to the Governor and a copy thereof shall be kept on file in the office of the Lieutenant Governor in a docket kept for that purpose.

(b) The Board of Pardons shall consist of the Lieutenant Governor who shall be chairman, the Attorney General and three members appointed by the Governor with the consent of a majority of the members elected to the Senate for terms of six years. The three members appointed by the Governor shall be residents of Pennsylvania. One shall be a crime victim, one a corrections expert and the third a doctor of medicine, psychiatrist or psychologist. The board shall keep records of its actions, which shall at all times be open for public inspection.

SECTION 10. INFORMATION FROM DEPARTMENT OFFICIALS. [58]

The Governor may require information in writing from the officers of the Executive Department, upon any subject relating to the duties of their respective offices.

SECTION 11. MESSAGES TO THE GENERAL ASSEMBLY.

He shall, from time to time, give to the General Assembly information of the state of the Commonwealth, and recommend to their consideration such measures as he may judge expedient.

SECTION 12. POWER TO CONVENE AND ADJOURN THE GENERAL ASSEMBLY.

He may, on extraordinary occasions, convene the General Assembly, and in case of disagreement between the two Houses, with respect to the time of adjournment, adjourn them to such time as he shall think proper, not exceeding four months. He shall have power to convene the Senate in extraordinary session by proclamation for the transaction of Executive business.

SECTION 13. WHEN LIEUTENANT GOVERNOR TO ACT AS GOVERNOR. [59]

In the case of the death, conviction on impeachment, failure to qualify or resignation of the Governor, the Lieutenant Governor shall become Governor for the remainder of the term and in the case of the disability of the Governor, the powers, duties and emoluments of the office shall devolve upon the Lieutenant Governor until the disability is removed.

SECTION 14. VACANCY IN OFFICE OF LIEUTENANT GOVERNOR. [60]

In case of the death, conviction on impeachment, failure to qualify or resignation of the Lieutenant Governor, or in case he should become Governor under section 13 of this article, the President *pro tempore* of the Senate shall become Lieutenant Governor for the remainder of the term. In case of the disability of the Lieutenant Governor, the powers, duties and emoluments of the office shall devolve upon the President *pro tempore* of the Senate until the disability is removed. Should there be no

Lieutenant Governor, the President *pro tempore* of the Senate shall become Governor if a vacancy shall occur in the office of Governor and in case of the disability of the Governor, the powers, duties and emoluments of the office shall devolve upon the President *pro tempore* of the Senate until the disability is removed. His seat as Senator shall become vacant whenever he shall become Governor and shall be filled by election as any other vacancy in the Senate.

SECTION 15. APPROVAL OF BILLS; VETOES.
Every bill which shall have passed both Houses shall be presented to the Governor; if he approves he shall sign it, but if he shall not approve he shall return it with his objections to the House in which it shall have originated, which House shall enter the objections at large upon their journal, and proceed to re-consider it. If after such re-consideration, two-thirds of all the members elected to that House shall agree to pass the bill, it shall be sent with the objections to the other House by which likewise it shall be re-considered, and if approved by two-thirds of all the members elected to that House it shall be a law; but in such cases the votes of both Houses shall be determined by yeas and nays, and the names of the members voting for and against the bill shall be entered on the journals of each House, respectively. If any bill shall not be returned by the Governor within ten days after it shall have been presented to him, the same shall be a law in like manner as if he had signed it, unless the General Assembly, by their adjournment, prevent its return, in which case it shall be a law, unless he shall file the same, with his objections, in the office of the Secretary of the Commonwealth, and give notice

thereof by public proclamation within 30 days after such adjournment.

SECTION 16. PARTIAL DISAPPROVAL OF APPROPRIATION BILLS.

The Governor shall have power to disapprove of any item or items of any bill, making appropriations of money, embracing distinct items, and the part or parts of the bill approved shall be the law, and the item or items of appropriation disapproved shall be void, unless re-passed according to the rules and limitations prescribed for the passage of other bills over the Executive veto.

SECTION 17. CONTESTED ELECTIONS OF GOVERNOR, LIEUTENANT GOVERNOR AND ATTORNEY GENERAL; WHEN SUCCEEDED. [61]

The Chief Justice of the Supreme Court shall preside upon the trial of any contested election of Governor, Lieutenant Governor or Attorney General and shall decide questions regarding the admissibility of evidence, and shall, upon request of the committee, pronounce his opinion upon other questions of law involved in the trial. The Governor, Lieutenant Governor and Attorney General shall exercise the duties of their respective offices until their successors shall be duly qualified.

SECTION 18. TERMS OF OFFICE OF AUDITOR GENERAL AND STATE TREASURER; NUMBER OF TERMS; ELIGIBILITY OF STATE TREASURER TO BECOME AUDITOR GENERAL. [62]

The terms of the Auditor General and of the State Treasurer shall each be four (4) years from the third Tuesday of January next ensuing his election. They shall be chosen by the qualified electors of the Commonwealth at general elections but shall not be eligible to serve continuously for more than two (2) successive terms. The State Treasurer shall rot be eligible to the office of Auditor General until four (4) years after he has been State Treasurer.

SECTION 19. STATE SEAL; COMMISSIONS. [63]

The present Great Seal of Pennsylvania shall be the seal of the State. All commissions shall be in the name and by authority of the Commonwealth of Pennsylvania, and be sealed with the State seal and signed by the Governor.

ARTICLE V
THE JUDICIARY [64]

SECTION

SECTION 1. UNIFIED JUDICIAL SYSTEM. [65]

The judicial power of the Commonwealth shall be vested in a unified judicial system consisting of the Supreme Court, the Superior Court, the Commonwealth Court, courts of common pleas, community courts, municipal courts in the City of Philadelphia, such other courts as may be provided by law and justices of the peace. All courts and justices of the peace and their jurisdiction shall be in this unified judicial system.

SECTION 2. SUPREME COURT.

The Supreme Court **(a)** shall be the highest court of the Commonwealth and in this court shall be reposed the supreme judicial power of the Commonwealth; **(b)** shall consist of seven justices, one of whom shall be the Chief Justice; and **(c)** shall have such jurisdiction as shall be provided by law.

SECTION 3. SUPERIOR COURT. [66]
The Superior Court shall be a statewide court, and shall consist of the number of judges, which shall be not less than seven judges, and have such jurisdiction as shall be provided by this Constitution or by the General Assembly. One of its judges shall be the president judge.

SECTION 4. COMMONWEALTH COURT.
The Commonwealth Court shall be a statewide court, and shall consist of the number of judges and have such jurisdiction as shall be provided by law. One of its judges shall be the president judge.

SECTION 5. COURTS OF COMMON PLEAS.
There shall be one court of common pleas for each judicial district
(a) having such divisions and consisting of such number of judges as shall be provided by law, one of whom shall be the president judge; and
(b) having unlimited original jurisdiction in all cases except as may otherwise be provided by law.

SECTION 6. COMMUNITY COURTS; PHILADELPHIA MUNICIPAL COURT. [67]
(a) In any judicial district a majority of the electors voting thereon may approve the establishment or discontinuance of a community court. Where a community court is approved, one community court

shall be established; its divisions, number of judges and jurisdiction shall be as provided by law.

(b) The question whether a community court shall be established or discontinued in any judicial district shall be placed upon the ballot in a primary election by petition which shall be in the form prescribed by the officer of the Commonwealth who under law shall have supervision over elections. The petition shall be filed with that officer and shall be signed by a number of electors equal to 5% of the total votes cast for all candidates for the office occupied by a single official for which the highest number of votes was cast in that judicial district at the last preceding general or municipal election. The manner of signing such petitions, the time of circulating them, the affidavits of the persons circulating them and all other details not contained herein shall be governed by the general laws relating to elections. The question shall not be placed upon the ballot in a judicial district more than once in any five-year period.

(c) In the City of Philadelphia there shall be a municipal court. The number of judges and the jurisdiction shall be as provided by law. This court shall exist so long as a community court has not been established or in the event one has been discontinued under this section.

SECTION 7. JUSTICES OF THE PEACE; MAGISTERIAL DISTRICTS.

(a) In any judicial district, other than the City of Philadelphia, where a community court has not been established or where one has been discontinued there shall be one justice of the peace in each magisterial district. The jurisdiction of the justice of the peace shall be as provided by law.

(b) The General Assembly shall by law establish classes of magisterial districts solely on the basis of population and population density and shall fix the salaries to be paid justices of the peace in each class. The number and boundaries of magisterial districts of each class within each judicial district shall be established by the Supreme Court or by the courts of common pleas under the direction of the Supreme Court as required for the efficient administration of justice within each magisterial district.

SECTION 8. OTHER COURTS.
The General Assembly may establish additional courts or divisions of existing courts, as needed, or abolish any statutory court or division thereof.

SECTION 9. RIGHT OF APPEAL. [68]
There shall be a right of appeal in all cases to a court of record from a court not of record; and there shall also be a right of appeal from a court of record or from an administrative agency to a court of record or to an appellate court, the selection of such court to be as provided by law; and there shall be such other rights of appeal as may be provided by law.

SECTION 10. JUDICIAL ADMINISTRATION. [69]
(a) The Supreme Court shall exercise general supervisory and administrative authority over all the courts and justices of the peace, including authority to temporarily assign judges and justices of the peace from one court or district to another as it deems appropriate.
(b) The Supreme Court shall appoint a court administrator and may appoint such subordinate

administrators and staff as may be necessary and proper for the prompt and proper disposition of the business of all courts and justices of the peace.

(c) The Supreme Court shall have the power to prescribe general rules governing practice, procedure and the conduct of all courts, justices of the peace and all officers serving process or enforcing orders, judgments or decrees of any court or justice of the peace, including the power to provide for assignment and reassignment of classes of actions or classes of appeals among the several courts as the needs of justice shall require, and for admission to the bar and to practice law, and the administration of all courts and supervision of all officers of the Judicial Branch, if such rules are consistent with this Constitution and neither abridge, enlarge nor modify the substantive rights of any litigant, nor affect the right of the General Assembly to determine the jurisdiction of any court or justice of the peace, nor suspend nor alter any statute of limitation or repose. All laws shall be suspended to the extent that they are inconsistent with rules prescribed under these provisions. Notwithstanding the provisions of this section, the General Assembly may by statute provide for the manner of testimony of child victims or child material witnesses in criminal proceedings, including the use of videotaped depositions or testimony by closed-circuit television.

(d) The Chief Justice and president judges of all courts with seven or less judges shall be the justice or judge longest in continuous service on their respective courts; and in the event of his resignation from this position the justice or judge next longest in continuous service shall be the Chief Justice or president judge. The president judges of all other courts shall be selected for five-year terms by the members of their respective courts. A Chief Justice or president judge may resign such position and remain a member of the court. In the event of a tie vote for office of president judge in a court which elects its president judge, the Supreme Court shall appoint as president judge one of the judges receiving the highest number of votes.

(e) Should any two or more justices or judges of the same court assume office at the same time, they shall cast lots forthwith for priority of commission, and certify the results to the Governor who shall issue their commissions accordingly.

SECTION 11. JUDICIAL DISTRICTS; BOUNDARIES. [70]

The number and boundaries of judicial districts shall be changed by the General Assembly only with the advice and consent of the Supreme Court.

SECTION 12. QUALIFICATIONS OF JUSTICES, JUDGES AND JUSTICES OF THE PEACE. [71]

(a) Justices, judges and justices of the peace shall be citizens of the Commonwealth. Justices and judges, except the judges of the traffic court in the City of Philadelphia, shall be members of the bar of the Supreme Court. Justices and judges of statewide courts, for a period of one year preceding their election or appointment and during their continuance in office, shall reside within the Commonwealth. Other judges and justices of the peace, for a period of one year preceding their election or appointment and during their continuance in office, shall reside within their respective districts, except as provided in this article for temporary assignments.

(b) Justices of the peace shall be members of the bar of the Supreme Court or shall complete a course of training and instruction in the duties of their respective offices and pass an examination prior to assuming office. Such courses and examinations shall be as provided by law.

SECTION 13. ELECTION OF JUSTICES, JUDGES AND JUSTICES OF THE PEACE; VACANCIES. [72]

(a) Justices, judges and justices of the peace shall be elected at the municipal election next preceding the commencement of their respective terms of office by the electors of the Commonwealth or the respective districts in which they are to serve.

(b) A vacancy in the office of justice, judge or justice of the peace shall be filled by appointment by the Governor. The appointment shall be with the advice and consent of two-thirds of the members elected to the Senate, except in the case of justices of the peace which shall be by a majority. The person so appointed shall serve for a term ending on the first Monday of January following the next municipal election more than ten months after the vacancy occurs or for the remainder of the unexpired term whichever is less, except in the case of persons selected as additional judges to the Superior Court, where the General Assembly may stagger and fix the length of the initial terms of such additional judges by reference to any of the first, second and third municipal elections more than ten months after the additional judges are selected. The manner by which any additional judges are selected shall be provided by this section for the filling of vacancies in judicial offices.

(c) The provisions of section 13(b) shall not apply either in the case of a vacancy to be filled by retention election as provided in section 15(b), or in the case of a vacancy created by failure of a justice or judge to file a declaration for retention election as provided in section 15(b). In the case of a vacancy occurring at the expiration of an appointive term under section 13(b), the vacancy shall be filled by election as provided in section 13(a).

(d) At the primary election in 1969, the electors of the Commonwealth may elect to have the justices and judges of the Supreme, Superior, Commonwealth and all other statewide courts appointed by the Governor from a list of persons qualified for the offices submitted to him by the Judicial Qualifications Commission. If a majority vote of those voting on the question is in favor of this method of appointment, then whenever any vacancy occurs thereafter for any reason in such court, the Governor shall fill the vacancy by appointment in the manner prescribed in this subsection. Such appointment shall not require the consent of the Senate.

(e) Each justice or judge appointed by the Governor under section 13(d) shall hold office for an initial term ending the first Monday of January following the next municipal election more than 24 months following the appointment.

SECTION 14. JUDICIAL QUALIFICATIONS COMMISSION. [73]

(a) Should the method of judicial selection be adopted as provided in Section 13(d), there shall be a Judicial Qualifications Commission, composed of four (4) non-lawyer electors appointed by the Governor and three (3) non-judge members of the bar of the Supreme Court appointed by the Supreme Court. No more than four (4) members shall be of the same political party. The members of the commission shall serve for terms of seven (7) years, with one (1) member being selected each year. The commission shall consider all names submitted to it and recommend to the Governor not fewer than ten nor more than twenty (20) of those qualified for each vacancy to be filled.

(b) During his term, no member shall hold a public office or public appointment for which he receives compensation, nor shall he hold office in a political party or political organization.

(c) A vacancy on the commission shall be filled by the appointing authority for the balance of the term.

SECTION 15. TENURE OF JUSTICES, JUDGES AND JUSTICES OF THE PEACE. [74]

(a) The regular term of office of justices and judges shall be ten (10) years and the regular term of office for judges of the municipal court in the City of Philadelphia and of justices of the peace shall be six (6) years. The tenure of any justice or judge shall not be affected by changes in judicial districts or by reduction in the number of judges.

(b) A justice or judge elected under Section 13(a), appointed under Section 13(d) or retained under this Section 15(b) may file a declaration of candidacy for retention election with the officer of the Commonwealth who under law shall have supervision over elections on or before the first Monday of January of the year preceding the year in which his term of office expires. If no declaration is filed, a vacancy shall exist upon the expiration of the term of office of such justice or judge, to be filled by election under Section 13(a) or by appointment under Section 13(d) if applicable. If a justice or judge files a declaration, his name shall be submitted to the electors without party designation, on a separate judicial ballot or in a separate column on voting machines, at the municipal election immediately preceding the expiration of the term of office of the justice or judge, to determine only the question whether he shall be retained in office. If a majority is against retention, a vacancy shall exist upon the expiration of his term of office, to be filled by appointment under section 13(b) or under section 13(d) if applicable. If a majority favors retention, the justice or judge shall serve for the regular term of office provided herein, unless sooner removed or retired. At the expiration of each term a justice or judge shall be eligible for retention as provided herein, subject only to the retirement provisions of this article.

SECTION 16. COMPENSATION AND RETIREMENT OF JUSTICES, JUDGES AND JUSTICES OF THE PEACE. [75]

(a) Justices, judges and justices of the peace shall be compensated by the Commonwealth as provided by law. Their compensation shall not be diminished during their terms of office, unless by law applying generally to all salaried officers of the Commonwealth.

(b) Justices, judges and justices of the peace shall be retired on the last day of the calendar year in which they attain the age of 75 years. Former and retired justices, judges and justices of the peace shall receive such compensation as shall be provided by law. Except as provided by law, no salary, retirement benefit or other compensation, present or deferred, shall be paid to any justice, judge or justice of the peace who, under section 18 or under Article VI, is suspended, removed or barred from holding judicial office for conviction of a felony or misconduct in office or conduct which prejudices the proper administration of justice or brings the judicial office into disrepute. **(c)** A former or retired justice or judge may, with his consent, be assigned by the Supreme Court on temporary judicial service as may be prescribed by rule of the Supreme Court.

SECTION 17. PROHIBITED ACTIVITIES. [76]

(a) Justices and judges shall devote full time to their judicial duties, and shall not engage in the practice of law, hold office in a political party or political organization, or hold an office or position of profit in the government of the United States, the Commonwealth or any municipal corporation or political subdivision thereof, except in the armed service of the United States or the Commonwealth.

(b) Justices and judges shall not engage in any activity prohibited by law and shall not violate any canon of legal or judicial ethics prescribed by the Supreme Court. Justices of the peace shall be governed by rules or canons which shall be prescribed by the Supreme Court.

(c) No justice, judge or justice of the peace shall be paid or accept for the performance of any judicial duty or for any service connected with his office, any fee, emolument or perquisite other than the salary and expenses provided by law.

(d) No duties shall be imposed by law upon the Supreme Court or any of the justices thereof or the Superior Court or any of the judges thereof, except such as are judicial, nor shall any of them exercise any power of appointment except as provided in this Constitution.

SECTION 18. SUSPENSION, REMOVAL, DISCIPLINE AND OTHER SANCTIONS. [77]

(a) There shall be an independent board within the Judicial Branch, known as the Judicial Conduct Board, the composition, powers and duties of which shall be as follows:

> **(1)** The board shall be composed of twelve (12) members, as follows: two (2) judges, other than senior judges, one (1) from the courts of common pleas and the other from either the Superior Court or the Commonwealth Court, one (1) justice of the peace who need not be a member of the bar of the Supreme Court, three (3) non-judge members of the bar of the Supreme Court and six (6) non-lawyer electors.

> **(2)** The judge from either the Superior Court or the Commonwealth Court, the justice of the peace, one (1) non-judge member of the bar of the Supreme Court and three (3) non-lawyer electors shall be appointed to the board by the Supreme Court. The judge from the courts of common pleas, two (2) non-judge members of the bar of the Supreme Court and three (3) non-lawyer electors shall be appointed to the board by the Governor.

> **(3)** Except for the initial appointees whose terms shall be provided by the schedule to this article, the members shall serve for terms of four (4) years. All members must be residents of this Commonwealth. No more than three (3) of the six (6) members appointed by the Supreme Court may be registered in the same political party. No more than three (3) of the six (6) members appointed by the Governor may be registered in the same political party. Membership of a judge or justice of the peace shall terminate if

the member ceases to hold the judicial position that qualified the member for the appointment. Membership shall terminate if a member attains a position that would have rendered the member ineligible for appointment at the time of the appointment. A vacancy shall be filled by the respective appointing authority for the remainder of the term to which the member was appointed. No member may serve more than four (4) consecutive years but may be reappointed after a lapse of one (1) year. The Governor shall convene the board for its first meeting. At that meeting and annually thereafter, the members of the board shall elect a chairperson. The board shall act only with the concurrence of a majority of its members.

(4) No member of the board, during the member's term, may hold office in a political party or political organization. Except for a judicial member, no member of the board, during the member's term, may hold a compensated public office or public appointment. All members shall be reimbursed for expenses necessarily incurred in the discharge of their official duties.

(5) The board shall prescribe general rules governing the conduct of members. A member may be removed by the board for a violation of the rules governing the conduct of members.

(6) The board shall appoint a chief counsel and other staff, prepare and administer its own budget as provided by law, exercise supervisory and administrative authority over all board staff and board functions, establish and promulgate its own rules of procedure, prepare and disseminate an annual report and take other actions as are necessary to ensure its efficient operation. The budget request of the board shall be made by the board as a separate item in the request submitted by the Supreme Court on behalf of the Judicial Branch to the General Assembly.

(7) The board shall receive and investigate complaints regarding judicial conduct filed by individuals or initiated by the board; issue subpoenas to compel testimony under oath of witnesses, including the subject of the investigation, and to compel the production of documents, books, accounts and other records relevant to the investigation; determine whether there is probable cause to file formal charges against a justice, judge or justice of the peace for conduct proscribed by this section; and present the case in support of the charges before the Court of Judicial Discipline.

(8) Complaints filed with the board or initiated by the board shall not be public information. Statements, testimony, documents, records or other information or evidence acquired by the board in the conduct of an investigation shall not be public information. A justice, judge or justice of the peace who is the subject of a complaint filed with the board or initiated by the board or of an investigation conducted by the board shall be apprised of the nature and content of the complaint and afforded an opportunity to respond fully to the complaint prior to any probable cause determination by the board. All proceedings of the board shall be confidential except when the subject of the investigation waives confidentiality. If, independent of any action by the board, the fact that an investigation by the board is in progress becomes a matter of public record, the board may, at the direction of the subject of the investigation, issue a statement to confirm that the investigation is in progress, to clarify the procedural aspects of the proceedings, to explain the rights of the subject of the investigation to a fair hearing without prejudgment or to provide the response of the subject of the investigation to the complaint. In acting to dismiss a complaint for lack of probable cause to file formal charges, the board may, at its discretion, issue a statement or report to the complainant or to the subject of the complaint, which may contain the identity of the complainant, the identity of the subject of the complaint, the contents and nature of the complaint, the actions taken in the conduct of the investigation and the results and conclusions of the investigation. The board may include with a report a copy of information or evidence acquired in the course of the investigation.

(9) If the board finds probable cause to file formal charges concerning mental or physical disability against a justice, judge or justice of the peace, the board shall so notify the subject of the charges and provide the subject with an opportunity to resign from judicial office or, when appropriate, to enter a rehabilitation program prior to the filing of the formal charges with the Court of Judicial Discipline.

(10) Members of the board and its chief counsel and staff shall be absolutely immune from suit for all conduct in the course of their official duties. No civil action or disciplinary complaint predicated upon the filing of a complaint or other documents with the board or testimony before the board may be maintained against any complainant, witness or counsel.

(b) There shall be a Court of Judicial Discipline, the composition, powers and duties of which shall be as follows:

(1) The court shall be composed of a total of eight (8) members as follows: three (3) judges other than senior judges from the courts of common pleas, the Superior Court or the Commonwealth Court, one (1) justice of the peace, two (2) non-judge members of the bar of the Supreme Court and two (2) non-lawyer electors. Two (2) judges, the justice of the peace and one (1) non-lawyer elector shall be appointed to the court by the Supreme Court. One (1) judge, the two (2) non-judge members of the bar of the Supreme Court and one (1) non-lawyer elector shall be appointed to the court by the Governor.

(2) Except for the initial appointees whose terms shall be provided by the schedule to this article, each member shall serve for a term of four (4) years; however, the member, rather than the member's successor, shall continue to participate in any hearing in progress at the end of the member's term. All members must be residents of this Commonwealth. No more than two (2) of the members appointed by the Supreme Court may be registered in the same political party. No more than two (2) of the members appointed by the Governor may be registered in the same political party. Membership of a judge or justice of the peace shall terminate if the judge or justice of the peace ceases to hold the judicial position that qualified the judge or justice of the peace for appointment. Membership shall terminate if a member attains a position that would have rendered that person ineligible for appointment at the time of the appointment. A vacancy on the court shall be filled by the respective appointing authority for the remainder of the term to which the member was appointed in the same manner in which the original appointment occurred. No member of the court may serve more than four (4) consecutive years but may be reappointed after a lapse of one (1) year.

(3) The court shall prescribe general rules governing the conduct of members. A member may be removed by the court for a violation of the rules of conduct prescribed by the court. No member, during the member's term of service, may hold office in any political party or political organization. Except for a judicial member, no member of the court, during the member's term of service, may hold a compensated public office or public appointment. All members of the court shall be reimbursed for expenses necessarily incurred in the discharge of their official duties.

(4) The court shall appoint staff and prepare and administer its own budget as provided by law and undertake actions needed to ensure its efficient operation. All actions of the court, including disciplinary action, shall require approval by a majority vote of the members of the court. The budget request of the court shall be made as a separate item in the request by the Supreme Court on behalf of the Judicial Branch to the General Assembly. The court shall adopt rules to govern the conduct of proceedings before the court.

(5) Upon the filing of formal charges with the court by the board, the court shall promptly schedule a hearing or hearings to determine whether a sanction should be imposed against a justice, judge or justice of the peace pursuant to the provisions of this section. The court shall be a court of record, with all the attendant duties and powers appropriate to its function. Formal charges filed with the court shall be a matter of public record. All hearings conducted by the court shall be public proceedings conducted pursuant to the rules adopted by the court and in accordance with the principles of due process and the law of evidence. Parties appearing before the court shall have a right to discovery pursuant to the rules adopted by the court and shall have the right to subpoena witnesses and to compel the production of documents, books, accounts and other records as relevant. The subject of the charges shall be presumed innocent in any proceeding before the court, and the board shall have the burden of proving the charges by clear and convincing evidence. All decisions of the court shall be in writing and shall contain findings of fact and conclusions of law. A decision of the court may order removal from office, suspension, censure or other discipline as authorized by this section and as warranted by the record.

(6) Members of the court and the court's staff shall be absolutely immune from suit for all conduct in the course of their official duties, and no civil action or disciplinary complaint predicated on testimony before the court may be maintained against any witness or counsel.

(c) Decisions of the court shall be subject to review as follows:

(1) A justice, judge or justice of the peace shall have the right to appeal a final adverse order of discipline of the court. A judge or justice of the peace shall have the right to appeal to the Supreme Court in a manner consistent with rules adopted by the Supreme Court; a justice shall have the right to appeal to a special tribunal composed of seven judges, other than senior judges, chosen by lot from the judges of the Superior Court and Commonwealth Court who do not sit on the Court of Judicial Discipline or the board, in a manner consistent with rules adopted by the Supreme Court. The special tribunal shall hear and decide the appeal in the same manner in which the Supreme Court would hear and decide an appeal from an order of the court.

(2) On appeal, the Supreme Court or special tribunal shall review the record of the proceedings of the court as follows: on the law, the scope of review is plenary; on the facts, the scope of review is clearly erroneous; and, as to sanctions, the scope of review is whether the sanctions imposed were lawful. The Supreme Court or special tribunal may revise or reject an order of the court upon a determination that the order did not sustain this standard of review; otherwise, the Supreme Court or special tribunal shall affirm the order of the court.

(3) An order of the court which dismisses a complaint against a judge or justice of the peace may be appealed by the board to the Supreme Court, but the appeal shall be limited to questions of law. An order of the court which dismisses a complaint against a justice of the

Supreme Court may be appealed by the board to a special tribunal in accordance with paragraph (1), but the appeal shall be limited to questions of law.

(4) No justice, judge or justice of the peace may participate as a member of the board, the court, a special tribunal or the Supreme Court in any proceeding in which the justice, judge or justice of the peace is a complainant, the subject of a complaint, a party or a witness.

(d) A justice, judge or justice of the peace shall be subject to disciplinary action pursuant to this section as follows:

(1) A justice, judge or justice of the peace may be suspended, removed from office or otherwise disciplined for conviction of a felony; violation of Section 17 of this article; misconduct in office; neglect or failure to perform the duties of office or conduct which prejudices the proper administration of justice or brings the judicial office into disrepute, whether or not the conduct occurred while acting in a judicial capacity or is prohibited by law; or conduct in violation of a canon or rule prescribed by the Supreme Court. In the case of a mentally or physically disabled justice, judge or justice of the peace, the court may enter an order of removal from office, retirement, suspension or other limitations on the activities of the justice, judge or justice of the peace as warranted by the record. Upon a final order of the court for suspension without pay or removal, prior to any appeal, the justice, judge or justice of the peace shall be suspended or removed from office; and the salary of the justice, judge or justice of the peace shall cease from the date of the order.

(2) Prior to a hearing, the court may issue an interim order directing the suspension, with or without pay, of any justice, judge or justice of the peace against whom formal charges have been filed with the court by the board or against whom has been filed an indictment or information charging a felony. An interim order under this paragraph shall not be considered a final order from which an appeal may be taken.

(3) A justice, judge or justice of the peace convicted of misbehavior in office by a court, disbarred as a member of the bar of the Supreme Court or removed under this section shall forfeit automatically his judicial office and thereafter be ineligible for judicial office.

(4) A justice, judge or justice of the peace who files for nomination for or election to any public office other than a judicial office shall forfeit automatically his judicial office.

(5) This section is in addition to and not in substitution for the provisions for impeachment for misbehavior in office contained in Article VI. No justice, judge or justice of the peace against whom impeachment proceedings are pending in the Senate shall exercise any of the duties of office until acquittal.

SCHEDULE TO JUDICIARY ARTICLE [78]

COURTS OTHER THAN IN THE CITY OF PHILADELPHIA AND ALLEGHENY COUNTY

GENERAL PROVISIONS

COURTS OTHER THAN IN THE CITY OF PHILADELPHIA AND ALLEGHENY COUNTY

SECTION 1. THE SUPREME COURT. [79]

The Supreme Court shall exercise all the powers and, until otherwise provided by law, jurisdiction now vested in the present Supreme Court and, until otherwise provided by law, the accused in all cases of felonious homicide shall have the right of appeal to the Supreme Court.

SECTION 2. THE SUPERIOR COURT. [80]

Until otherwise provided by law, the Superior Court shall exercise all the jurisdiction now vested in the present Superior Court. The present terms of all judges of the Superior Court
which would otherwise expire on the first Monday of January in an odd-numbered year shall be extended to expire in the even-numbered year next following.

SECTION 3. COMMONWEALTH COURT.

The Commonwealth Court shall come into existence on January 1, 1970. Notwithstanding anything to the contrary in this article, the General Assembly shall stagger the initial terms of judges of the Commonwealth Court.

SECTION 4. THE COURTS OF COMMON PLEAS. [81]

Until otherwise provided by law, the several courts of common pleas shall exercise the jurisdiction now vested in the present courts of common pleas. The courts of *oyer* and *terminer* and general jail delivery, quarter sessions of the peace, and orphans' courts are abolished and the several courts of common pleas shall also exercise the jurisdiction of these courts. Orphans' courts in judicial districts having separate orphans' courts shall become orphans' court divisions of the courts of common pleas and the court of common pleas in those judicial districts shall exercise the jurisdiction presently exercised by the separate orphans' courts through their respective orphans' court division.

SECTION 5. ORPHANS' COURT JUDGES.

In those judicial districts having separate orphans' courts, the present judges thereof shall become judges of the orphans' court division of the court of common pleas and the present president judge shall become the president judge of the orphans' court division of the court of common pleas for the remainder of his term without diminution in salary.

SECTION 6. COURTS OF COMMON PLEAS IN MULTI-COUNTY JUDICIAL DISTRICTS.

Courts of common pleas in multi-county judicial districts are abolished as separate courts and are hereby constituted as branches of the single court of common pleas established under this article in each such judicial district.

SECTION 7. COMMUNITY COURTS.

In a judicial district which establishes a community court, a person serving as a justice of the peace at such time:

(a) May complete his term exercising the jurisdiction provided by law and with the compensation provided by law, and

(b) Upon completion of his term, his office is abolished and no judicial function of the kind heretofore exercised by a justice of the peace shall thereafter be exercised other than by the community court.

JUSTICES, JUDGES AND JUSTICES OF THE PEACE

SECTION 8. JUSTICES, JUDGES AND JUSTICES OF THE PEACE.

Notwithstanding any provision in the article, a present justice, judge or justice of the peace may complete his term of office.

SECTION 9. ASSOCIATE JUDGES.

The office of associate judge not learned in the law is abolished, but a present associate judge may complete his term.

SECTION 10. RETENTION ELECTION OF PRESENT JUSTICES AND JUDGES.

A present judge who was originally elected to office and seeks retention in the 1969 municipal election and is otherwise eligible may file his declaration of candidacy by February 1, 1969.

SECTION 11. SELECTION OF PRESIDENT JUDGES. [82]

(a) Except in the City of Philadelphia, Section 10(d) of the article shall become effective upon the expiration of the term of the present president judge, or upon earlier vacancy.

(b) Notwithstanding Section 10(d) of the article the president judge of the Superior Court shall be the judge longest in continuous service on such court if such judge was a member of such court on the first (1st) Monday of January 1977. If no such judge exists or is willing to serve as president judge the president judge shall be selected as provided by this article.

MAGISTRATES, ALDERMEN AND JUSTICES OF THE PEACE AND MAGISTERIAL DISTRICTS OTHER THAN IN THE CITY OF PHILADELPHIA

SECTION 12. MAGISTRATES, ALDERMEN AND JUSTICES OF THE PEACE.

An alderman, justice of the peace or magistrate:

(a) May complete his term, exercising the jurisdiction provided by law and with the method of compensation provided by law prior to the adoption of this article;

(b) Shall be deemed to have taken and passed the examination required by this article for justices of the peace if he has completed one full term of office before creation of a magisterial district, and

(c) At the completion of his term, his office is abolished.

(d) Except for officers completing their terms, after the first Monday in January, 1970, no judicial function of the kind heretofore exercised by these officers, by mayors and like officers in municipalities shall be exercised by any officer other than the one justice of the peace elected or appointed to serve in that magisterial district.

SECTION 13. MAGISTERIAL DISTRICTS. [83]

So that the provisions of this article regarding the establishment of magisterial districts and the instruction and examination of justices of the peace may be self-executing, until otherwise provided by law in a manner agreeable to this article, the following provisions shall be in force:

(a) The Supreme Court or the courts of common pleas under the direction of the Supreme Court shall fix the number and boundaries of magisterial districts of each class within each judicial district by January 1, 1969, and these magisterial districts, except where a community court has been adopted, shall come into existence on January 1, 1970, the justices of the peace thereof to be elected at the municipal election in 1969. These justices of the peace shall retain no fine, costs or any other sum that shall be delivered into their hands for the performance of any judicial duty or for any service connected with their offices, but shall remit the same to the Commonwealth, county, municipal subdivision, school district or otherwise as may be provided by law.

(b) Classes of magisterial districts.

(i)   Magisterial districts of the first class shall have a population density of more than 5,000 persons per square mile and a population of not less than 65,000 persons.

(ii) Magisterial districts of the second class shall have a population density of between 1,000 and 5,000 persons per square mile and a population of between 20,000 persons and 65,000 persons.

(iii) Magisterial districts of the third class shall have a population density of between 200 and 1,000 persons per square mile and a population of between 12,000 persons and 20,000 persons.

(iv) Magisterial districts of the fourth class shall have a population density of between 70 and 200 persons per square mile and a population of between 7,500 persons and 12,000 persons.

(v) Magisterial districts of the fifth class shall have a population density of under 70 persons per square mile and a population of between 4,000 persons and 7,500 persons.

(c) Salaries of justices of the peace.

The salaries of the justices of the peace shall be as follows:

(i)   In first class magisterial districts, $12,000 per year,

(ii) In second class magisterial districts, $10,000 per year,

(iii) In third class magisterial districts, $8,000 per year,

(iv) In fourth and fifth class magisterial districts, $5,000 per year.

(v) The salaries here fixed shall be paid by the State Treasurer and for such payment this article and schedule shall be sufficient warrant.

(d) Course of training, instruction and examination. The course of training and instruction and examination in civil and criminal law and procedure for a justice of the peace shall be devised by the Department of Public Instruction, and it shall administer this course and examination to insure that justices of the peace are competent to perform their duties.

SECTION 14. MAGISTERIAL DISTRICTS.

Effective immediately upon establishment of magisterial districts and until otherwise prescribed the civil and criminal procedural rules relating to venue shall apply to magisterial districts; all proceedings before aldermen, magistrates and justices of the peace shall be brought in and only in a magisterial district in which occurs an event which would give rise to venue in a court of record; the court of common pleas upon its own motion or on application at any stage of proceedings shall transfer any proceeding in any magisterial district to the justice of the peace for the magisterial district in which proper venue lies.

PROTHONOTARIES AND CLERKS
OTHER THAN IN THE CITY OF PHILADELPHIA

SECTION 15. PROTHONOTARIES, CLERKS OF COURTS, CLERKS OF ORPHANS' COURTS.

Until otherwise provided by law, the offices of prothonotary and clerk of courts shall become the offices of prothonotary and clerk of courts of the court of common pleas of the judicial district, and in multi-county judicial districts of their county's branch of the court of common pleas, and the clerk of the orphans' court in a judicial district now having a separate orphans' court shall become the clerk of the orphans' court division of the court of common pleas, and these officers shall continue to perform the duties of the office and to maintain and be responsible for the records, books and dockets as heretofore. In judicial districts where the clerk of the orphans' court is not the register of wills, he shall continue to perform the duties of the office and to maintain and be responsible for the records, books and dockets as heretofore until otherwise provided by law.

THE CITY OF PHILADELPHIA

SECTION 16. COURTS AND JUDGES. [84]

(a) Until otherwise provided by law: the court of common pleas shall consist of a trial division, orphans' court division and family court division.

(b) The judges of the court of common pleas shall become judges of the trial division of the court of common pleas provided for in this article and their tenure shall not otherwise be affected.

(c) The judges of the county court shall become judges of the family court division of the court of common pleas and their tenure shall not otherwise be affected.

(d) The judges of the orphans' court shall become judges of the orphans' court division of the court of common pleas and their tenure shall not otherwise be affected.

(e) As designated by the Governor, twenty-two (22) of the present magistrates shall become judges of the municipal court and six (6) shall become judges of the traffic court, and their tenure shall not otherwise be affected.

(f) One of the judges of the court of common pleas shall be president judge and he shall be selected in the manner provided in Section 10(d) of this article.

He shall be the administrative head of the court and shall supervise the court's judicial business.

(g) Each division of the court of common pleas shall be presided over by an administrative judge, who shall be one of its judges and shall be elected for a term of five (5) years by a majority vote of the judges of that division. He shall assist the president judge in supervising the judicial business of the court and shall be responsible to him. Subject to the foregoing, the judges of the court of common pleas shall prescribe rules defining the duties of the administrative judges. The president judge shall have the power to assign judges from each division to each other division of the court when required to expedite the business of the court.

(h) Until all members of the municipal court are members of the bar of the Supreme Court, the president judge of the court of common pleas shall appoint one of the judges of the municipal court as president judge for a five-year term or at the pleasure of the president judge of the court of common pleas. The president judge of the municipal court shall be eligible to succeed himself as president judge for any number of terms and shall be the administrative head of that court and shall supervise the judicial business of the court. He shall promulgate all administrative rules and regulations and make all judicial assignments. The president judge of the court of common pleas may assign temporarily judges of the municipal court who are members of the bar of the Supreme Court to the court of common pleas when required to expedite the business of the court.

(i) The Governor shall appoint one of the judges of the traffic court as president judge for a term of five (5) years or at the pleasure of the Governor. The president judge of the traffic court shall be eligible to succeed himself as president judge for any number of terms, shall be the executive and administrative head of the traffic court, and shall supervise the judicial business of the court, shall promulgate all administrative rules and regulations, and shall make all judicial assignments.

(j) The exercise of all supervisory and administrative powers detailed in this section 16 shall be subject to the supervisory and administrative control of the Supreme Court.

(k) The prothonotary shall continue to exercise the duties of that office for the trial division of the court of common pleas and for the municipal court.

(l) The clerk of quarter sessions shall continue to exercise the duties of that office for the trial division of the court of common pleas and for the municipal court.

(m) That officer serving as clerk to the county court shall continue to exercise the duties of that office for the family division of the court of common pleas.

(n) The register of wills shall serve ex officio as clerk of the orphans' court division of the court of common pleas.

(o) The court of common pleas shall have unlimited original jurisdiction in all cases except those cases assigned by this schedule to the municipal court and to the traffic court. The court of common pleas shall have all the jurisdiction now vested in the court of common pleas, the court of *oyer* and *terminer* and general jail delivery, courts of quarter sessions of the peace, orphans' court, and county court. Jurisdiction in all of the foregoing cases shall be exercised through the trial division of the court of common pleas except in those cases which are assigned by this schedule to the orphans' court and family court divisions of the court of common pleas. The court of common pleas through the trial division shall also hear and determine appeals from the municipal court and traffic court.

(p) The court of common pleas through the orphans' court division shall exercise the jurisdiction heretofore exercised by the orphans' court.

(q) The court of common pleas through the family court division of the court of common pleas shall exercise jurisdiction in the following matters:

(i) Domestic Relations: desertion or nonsupport of wives, children and indigent parents, including children born out of wedlock; proceedings for custody of children; divorce and annulment and property matters relating thereto.

(ii) Juvenile Matters: dependent, delinquent and neglected children and children under 18 years of age, suffering from epilepsy, nervous or mental defects, incorrigible, runaway and disorderly minors 18 to 20 years of age and preliminary hearings in criminal cases where the victim is a juvenile.

(iii) Adoptions and Delayed Birth Certificates.

(r) The municipal court shall have jurisdiction in the following matters:

(i) Committing magistrates' jurisdiction in all criminal matters.

(ii) All summary offenses, except those under the motor vehicle laws. *(iii)* All criminal offenses for which no prison term may be imposed or which are punishable by a term of imprisonment of not more than two years, and indictable offenses under the motor vehicle laws for which no prison term may be imposed or punishable by a term of imprisonment of not more than three years. In these cases, the defendant shall have no right of trial by jury in that court, but he shall have the right of appeal for trial de novo including the right to trial by jury to the trial division of the court of

common pleas. Until there are a sufficient number of judges who are members of the bar of the Supreme Court serving in the municipal court to handle such matters, the trial division of the court of common pleas shall have concurrent jurisdiction over such matters, the assignment of cases to the respective courts to be determined by rule prescribed by the president judge of the court of common pleas. *(iv)* Matters arising under The Landlord and Tenant Act of 1951. *(v)* All civil claims involving less than $500. In these cases, the parties shall have no right of trial by jury in that court but shall have the right of appeal for a trial de novo including the right to trial by jury to the trial division of the court of common pleas, it being the purpose of this subsection to establish an expeditious small claims procedure whereby it shall not be necessary for the litigants to obtain counsel. This limited grant of civil jurisdiction shall be co-extensive with the civil jurisdiction of the trial division of the court of common pleas. *(vi)* As commissioners to preside at arraignments, fix and accept bail, issue warrants and perform duties of a similar nature. The grant of jurisdiction under clauses (iii) and (v) of this subsection may be exercised only by those judges who are members of the bar of the Supreme Court.

(s) The traffic court shall have exclusive jurisdiction of all summary offenses under the motor vehicle laws.

(t) The courts of *oyer* and *terminer* and general jail delivery, quarter sessions of the peace, the county court, the orphans' court and the ten separate courts of common pleas are abolished and their jurisdiction and powers shall be exercised by the court of common pleas provided for in this article through the divisions established by this schedule.

(u) The office of magistrate, the board of magistrates and the present traffic court are abolished.

(v) Those judges appointed to the municipal court in accordance with subsection (e) of this section who are not members of the bar of the Supreme Court shall be eligible to complete their present terms and to be elected to and serve for one additional term, but not thereafter.

(w) The causes, proceedings, books, dockets and records of the abolished courts shall become those of the court or division thereof to which, under this schedule, jurisdiction of the proceedings or matters concerned has been transferred, and that court or division thereof shall determine and conclude such proceedings as if it had assumed jurisdiction in the first instance.

(x) The present president judges of the abolished courts and chief magistrate shall continue to receive the compensation to which they are now entitled as president judges and chief magistrate until the end of their present terms as president judges and chief magistrate respectively.

(y) The offices of prothonotary and register of wills in the City of Philadelphia shall no longer be considered constitutional offices under this article, but their powers and functions shall continue as at present until these offices are covered in the Home Rule Charter by a referendum in the manner provided by law.

(z) If a community court is established in the City of Philadelphia, a person serving as a judge of the municipal or traffic court at that time:

    (i)   Notwithstanding the provisions of subsection (v) of this section, may complete his term exercising the jurisdiction provided by law and with the compensation provided by law; and

(ii) At the completion of his term, his office is abolished and no jurisdiction of the kind exercised by those officers immediately after the effective date of this article and schedule shall thereafter be exercised other than by the community court.

ALLEGHENY COUNTY

SECTION 17. COURTS. [85]

Until otherwise provided by law:

(a) The court of common pleas shall consist of a trial division, an orphans' court division and a family court division; the courts of *oyer* and *terminer* and general jail delivery and quarter sessions of the peace, the county court, the orphans' court, and the juvenile court are abolished and their present jurisdiction shall be exercised by the court of common pleas. Until otherwise provided by rule of the court of common pleas and, except as otherwise provided in this schedule, the court of common pleas shall exercise the jurisdiction of the present court of common pleas and the present county court through the trial division. Until otherwise provided by rule of the court of common pleas, the jurisdiction of the present orphans' court, except as otherwise provided in this schedule, shall be exercised by the court of common pleas through the orphans' court division.

(b) Until otherwise provided by rule of the court of common pleas, the court of common pleas shall exercise jurisdiction in the following matters through the family court division:

(i) Domestic Relations: Desertion or nonsupport of wives, children and indigent parents, including children born out of wedlock; proceedings, including habeas corpus, for custody of children; divorce and annulment and property matters relating thereto.

(ii) Juvenile Matters: All matters now within the jurisdiction of the juvenile court.

(iii) Adoptions and Delayed Birth Certificates.

18. JUDGES. [86]

Until otherwise provided by law, the present judges of the court of common pleas shall continue to act as the judges of that court; the present judges of the county court shall become judges of the court of common pleas; the present judges of the orphans' court shall become judges of the orphans' court division of the court of common pleas; the present judges of the juvenile court shall become judges of the family court division of the court of common pleas.

SECTION 19. PRESIDENT JUDGES.

The present president judge of the court of common pleas may complete his term as president judge; the present president judge of the orphans' court shall be the president judge of the orphans' court division of the court of common pleas for the remainder of his term as president judge, and the present president judge of the county court shall be the president judge of the family court division of the court of common pleas for the remainder of his term as president judge, all these without diminution of salary as president judge. The president judge of the trial division shall be selected pursuant to section 20 of this schedule.

SECTION 20. PRESIDENT JUDGES; COURT DIVISIONS. [87]

Until otherwise provided by law, the trial division, the orphans' court division and the family court division of the court of common pleas shall each be presided over by a president judge, who shall be one of the judges of such division and shall be elected for a term of five years by a majority vote of the judges of that division. He shall assist the president judge of the court of common pleas in supervising the judicial business of the court and shall be responsible to him. Subject to the foregoing, the judges of the court of common pleas shall prescribe rules defining the duties of the president judges. The president judge of the court of common pleas shall have the power to assign judges from one division to another division of the court when required to expedite the business of the court. The exercise of these supervisory and administrative powers, however, shall be subject to the supervisory and administrative powers of the Supreme Court.

THE CITY OF PITTSBURGH

SECTION 21. INFERIOR COURTS. [88]

Upon the establishment of magisterial districts pursuant to this article and schedule, and unless otherwise provided by law, the police magistrates, including those serving in the traffic court, the housing court and the city court shall continue as at present. Such magistrates shall be part of the unified judicial system and shall be subject to the general supervisory and administrative authority of the Supreme Court. Such magistrates shall be subject to the provisions of this article and schedule regarding educational requirements and prohibited activities of justices of the peace.

CAUSES, PROCEEDINGS, BOOKS AND RECORDS

SECTION 22. CAUSES, PROCEEDINGS, BOOKS AND RECORDS.

All causes and proceedings pending in any abolished court or office of the justice of the peace shall be determined and concluded by the court to which jurisdiction of the proceedings has been transferred under this schedule and all books, dockets and records of any abolished court or office of the justice of the peace shall become those of the court to which, under this schedule, jurisdiction of the proceedings concerned has been transferred.

COMMISSION AND BOARD

SECTION 23. JUDICIAL QUALIFICATIONS COMMISSION. [89]

The selection of the first members of the Judicial Qualifications Commission provided for in Section 14 (a) of this article shall be made as follows: The Governor shall appoint the four (4) non-lawyer members for terms of, respectively, one (1) year, three (3) years, five (5) years and seven (7) years, no more than two (2) of whom shall be members of the same political party. The Supreme Court shall appoint the three (3) non-judge members of the bar of the Supreme Court of Pennsylvania for terms, respectively, of two (2) years, four (4) years and six (6) years, no more than two (2) of whom shall be members of the same political party.

SECTION 24. JUDICIAL DISCIPLINE. 90

(a) The members of the Judicial Inquiry and Review Board shall vacate their offices ninety (90) days after the adoption of the amendment to Section 18 of this article, and all proceedings pending before the Judicial Inquiry and Review Board and all records shall be transferred to the Judicial Conduct Board for further proceedings.

(b) Of the members initially appointed to the Judicial Conduct Board, the judge appointed by the Supreme Court shall serve a four (4) year term, and the judge appointed by the Governor shall serve a three (3) year term. The justice of the peace initially appointed shall serve a two (2) year term. Of the three (3) non-judge members of the bar of the Supreme Court initially appointed, the first appointed by the Governor shall serve a three (3) year term, the next appointed by the Governor shall serve a two (2) year term, and the non-judge member of the bar of the Supreme Court appointed by the Supreme Court shall serve a one (1) year term. Of the six (6) non-lawyer electors initially appointed, the first appointed by the Governor and the first appointed by the Supreme Court shall serve a four (4) year term, the next appointed by the Governor and the next appointed by the Supreme Court shall serve a three (3) year term, and the next appointed by the Governor and the next appointed by the Supreme Court shall serve a two (2) year term.

(c) Of the three (3) judges initially appointed to the Court of Judicial Discipline, the first appointed by the Supreme Court shall serve a four (4) year term, the next appointed by the Supreme Court shall serve a three (3) year term, and the judge appointed by the Governor shall serve a two (2) year term. The justice of the peace initially appointed shall serve a one (1) year term. Of the non-judge members of the bar initially appointed, the first appointed shall serve a four (4) year term, and the next appointed shall serve a three (3) year term. Of the two (2) non-lawyer electors initially appointed, the non-lawyer elector appointed by the Governor shall serve a three (3) year term, and the non-lawyer elector appointed by the Supreme Court shall serve a two (2) year term.

GENERAL PROVISIONS

25. DISPENSING WITH TRIAL BY JURY. [91]
Until otherwise provided by law, the parties, by agreement filed, may in any civil case dispense with trial by jury, and submit the decision of such case to the court having jurisdiction thereof, and such court shall hear and determine the same; and the judgment thereon shall be subject to writ of error as in other cases.

SECTION 26. WRITS OF CERTIORARI.
Unless and until changed by rule of the Supreme Court, in addition to the right of appeal under section 9 of this article, the judges of the courts of common pleas, within their respective judicial districts, shall have power to issue writs of certiorari to the municipal court in the City of Philadelphia, justices of the peace and inferior courts not of record and to cause their proceedings to be brought before them, and right and justice to be done.

SECTION 27. JUDICIAL DISTRICTS. [92]
Until changed in accordance with Section 11 of this article, the number and boundaries of judicial districts shall remain as at present.

SECTION 28. REFERENDUM. [93]

The officer of the Commonwealth who under law shall have supervision over elections shall cause the question provided for in section 13(d) of this article to be placed on the ballot in the 1969 primary election throughout the Commonwealth.

SECTION 29. PERSONS SPECIALLY ADMITTED BY LOCAL RULES.

Any person now specially admitted to practice may continue to practice in the court of common pleas or in that division of the court of common pleas and the municipal court in the City of Philadelphia which substantially includes the practice for which such person was previously specially admitted.

ARTICLE VI [94]
PUBLIC OFFICERS

SECTION 1. SELECTION OF OFFICERS NOT OTHERWISE PROVIDED FOR IN CONSTITUTION. [95]

All officers, whose selection is not provided for in this Constitution, shall be elected or appointed as may be directed by law.

SECTION 2. INCOMPATIBLE OFFICES. [96]

No member of Congress from this State, nor any person holding or exercising any office or appointment of trust or profit under the United States, shall at the same time hold or exercise any office in this State to which a salary, fees or perquisites shall be attached. The General Assembly may by law declare what offices are incompatible.

SECTION 3. OATH OF OFFICE. [97]

Senators, Representatives and all judicial, State and county officers shall, before entering on the duties of their respective offices, take and subscribe the following oath or affirmation before a person authorized to administer oaths.

101

"I do solemnly swear (or affirm) that I will support, obey and defend the Constitution of the United States and the Constitution of this Commonwealth and that I will discharge the duties of my office with fidelity."

The oath or affirmation shall be administered to a member of the Senate or to a member of the House of Representatives in the hall of the House to which he shall have been elected. Any person refusing to take the oath or affirmation shall forfeit his office.

SECTION 4. POWER OF IMPEACHMENT. [98]
The House of Representatives shall have the sole power of impeachment.

SECTION 5. TRIAL OF IMPEACHMENTS. [99]
All impeachments shall be tried by the Senate. When sitting for that purpose the Senators shall be upon oath or affirmation. No person shall be convicted without the concurrence of two-thirds (2/3) of the members present.

SECTION 6. OFFICERS LIABLE TO IMPEACHMENT. [100]
The Governor and all other civil officers shall be liable to impeachment for any misbehavior in office, but judgment in such cases shall not extend further than to removal from office and disqualification to hold any office of trust or profit under this Commonwealth. The person accused, whether convicted or acquitted, shall nevertheless be liable to indictment, trial, judgment and punishment according to law.

SECTION 7. REMOVAL OF CIVIL OFFICERS. [101]

All civil officers shall hold their offices on the condition that they behave themselves well while in office, and shall be removed on conviction of misbehavior in office or of any infamous crime. Appointed civil officers, other than judges of the courts of record, may be removed at the pleasure of the power by which they shall have been appointed. All civil officers elected by the people, except the Governor, the Lieutenant Governor, members of the General Assembly and judges of the courts of record, shall be removed by the Governor for reasonable cause, after due notice and full hearing, on the address of two-thirds of the Senate.

ARTICLE VII
ELECTIONS [102]

Section

SECTION 1. QUALIFICATIONS OF ELECTORS. [103]

Every citizen 21 years of age, possessing the following qualifications, shall be entitled to vote at all elections subject, however, to such laws requiring and regulating the registration of electors as the General Assembly may enact.

1. He or she shall have been a citizen of the United States at least one month.

2. He or she shall have resided in the State 90 days immediately preceding the election.

3. He or she shall have resided in the election district where he or she shall offer to vote at least 60 days immediately preceding the election, except that if qualified to vote in an election district prior to removal of residence, he or she may, if a resident of Pennsylvania, vote in the election district from which he or she removed his or her residence within 60 days preceding the election.

SECTION 2. GENERAL ELECTION DAY. [104]

The general election shall be held biennially on the Tuesday next following the first Monday of November in each even-numbered year, but the General Assembly may by law fix a different day, two-thirds (2/3) of all the members of each House consenting thereto: Provided, That such election shall always be held in an even-numbered year.

SECTION 3. MUNICIPAL ELECTION DAY; OFFICES TO BE FILLED ON ELECTION DAYS. [105]

All judges elected by the electors of the State at large may be elected at either a general or municipal election, as circumstances may require. All elections for judges of the courts for the several judicial districts, and for county, city, ward, borough, and township officers, for regular terms of service, shall be held on the municipal election day; namely, the Tuesday next following the first Monday of November in each odd-numbered year, but the General Assembly may by law fix a different day, two-thirds (2/3) of all the members of each House consenting thereto: Provided, That such elections shall be held in an odd-numbered year: Provided further, That all judges for the courts of the several judicial districts holding office at the present time, whose terms of office may end in an odd-numbered year, shall continue to hold their offices until the first Monday of January in the next succeeding even-numbered year.

SECTION 4. METHOD OF ELECTIONS; SECRECY IN VOTING.[106]

All elections by the citizens shall be by ballot or by such other method as may be prescribed by law: Provided, That secrecy in voting be preserved.

SECTION 5. ELECTORS PRIVILEGED FROM ARREST.

Electors shall in all cases except treason, felony and breach or surety of the peace, be privileged from arrest during their attendance on elections and in going to and returning therefrom.

SECTION 6. ELECTION AND REGISTRATION LAWS. [107]

All laws regulating the holding of elections by the citizens, or for the registration of electors, shall be uniform throughout the State, except that laws regulating and requiring the registration of electors may be enacted to apply to cities only, provided that such laws be uniform for cities of the same class, and except further, that the General Assembly shall by general law, permit the use of voting machines, or other mechanical devices for registering or recording and computing the vote, at all elections or primaries, in any county, city, borough, incorporated town or township of the Commonwealth, at the option of the electors of such county, city, borough, incorporated town or township, without being obliged to require the use of such voting machines or mechanical devices in any other county, city, borough, incorporated town or township, under such regulations with reference thereto as the General Assembly may from time to time prescribe. The General Assembly may, from time to time, prescribe the number and duties of election officers in any political subdivision of the Commonwealth in which voting machines or other mechanical devices authorized by this section may be used.

SECTION 7. BRIBERY OF ELECTORS. [108]

Any person who shall give, or promise or offer to give, to an elector, any money, reward or other valuable consideration for his vote at an election, or for withholding the same, or who shall give or promise to give such consideration to any other person or party for such elector's vote or for the withholding thereof, and any elector who shall receive or agree to receive, for himself or for another, any money, reward or other valuable consideration for his vote at an election, or for withholding the same, shall thereby forfeit the right to vote at such election, and any elector whose right to vote shall be challenged for such cause before the election officers, shall be required to swear or affirm that the matter of the challenge is untrue before his vote shall be received.

SECTION 8. WITNESSES IN CONTESTED ELECTIONS. [109]

In trials of contested elections and in proceedings for the investigation of elections, no person shall be permitted to withhold his testimony upon the ground that it may criminate himself or subject him to public infamy; but such testimony shall not afterwards be used against him in any judicial proceedings except for perjury in giving such testimony.

SECTION 9. FIXING ELECTION DISTRICTS. [110]

Townships and wards of cities or boroughs shall form or be divided into election districts of compact and contiguous territory and their boundaries fixed and changed in such manner as may be provided by law.

SECTION 10. VIVA VOCE ELECTIONS. [111]
All elections by persons in a representative capacity shall be *viva voce* or by automatic recording device publicly indicating how each person voted.

SECTION 11. ELECTION OFFICERS. [112]
District election boards shall consist of a judge and two (2) inspectors, who shall be chosen at municipal elections for such terms as may be provided by law. Each elector shall have the right to vote for the judge and one inspector, and each inspector shall appoint one (1) clerk. The first election board for any new district shall be selected, and vacancies in election boards filled, as shall be provided by law. Election officers shall be privileged from arrest upon days of election, and while engaged in making up and transmitting returns, except upon warrant of a court of record or judge thereof, for an election fraud, for felony, or for wanton breach of the peace. In cities they may claim exemption from jury duty during their terms of service.

SECTION 12. DISQUALIFICATIONS FOR SERVICE AS ELECTION OFFICER. [113]
No persons shall be qualified to serve as an election officer who shall hold, or shall within two months have held any office, appointment or employment in or under the government of the United States, or of this State, or of any city, or county, or of any municipal board, commission or trust in any city, save only notaries public and persons in the National

Guard or in a reserve component of the armed forces of the United States; nor shall any election officer be eligible to any civil office to be filled at an election at which he shall serve, save only to such subordinate municipal or local offices, below the grade of city or county offices, as shall be designated by general law.

SECTION 13. CONTESTED ELECTIONS. [114]

The trial and determination of contested elections of electors of President and Vice-President, members of the General Assembly, and of all public officers, whether State, judicial, municipal or local, and contests involving questions submitted to the electors at any election shall be by the courts of law, or by one or more of the law judges thereof. The General Assembly shall, by general law, designate the courts and judges by whom the several classes of election contests shall be tried, and regulate the manner of trial and all matters incident thereto; but no such law assigning jurisdiction, or regulating its exercise, shall apply to any contest arising out of an election held before its passage.

SECTION 14. ABSENTEE VOTING. [115]

(a) The Legislature shall, by general law, provide a manner in which, and the time and place at which, qualified electors who may, on the occurrence of any election, be absent from the municipality of their residence, because their duties, occupation or business require them to be elsewhere or who, on the occurrence of any election, are unable to attend at their proper polling places because of illness or physical disability or who will not attend a polling place because of the observance of a religious holiday or who cannot vote because of election day duties, in the case of a county employee, may vote, and for the return and canvass of their votes in the election district in which they respectively reside.

(b) For purposes of this section, "municipality" means a city, borough, incorporated town, township or any similar general purpose unit of government which may be created by the General Assembly.

ARTICLE VIII [116]
TAXATION AND FINANCE

SECTION 1. UNIFORMITY OF TAXATION. [117]

All taxes shall be uniform, upon the same class of subjects, within the territorial limits of the authority levying the tax, and shall be levied and collected under general laws.

SECTION 2. EXEMPTIONS AND SPECIAL PROVISIONS. [118]

(a) The General Assembly may by law exempt from taxation:

(i) Actual places of regularly stated religious worship;

(ii) Actual places of burial, when used or held by a person or organization deriving no private or corporate profit therefrom and no substantial part of whose activity consists of selling personal property in connection therewith;

(iii) That portion of public property which is actually and regularly used for public purposes;

(iv) That portion of the property owned and occupied by any branch, post or camp of honorably discharged servicemen or servicewomen which is actually and regularly used for benevolent, charitable or patriotic purposes; and

(v) Institutions of purely public charity, but in the case of any real property tax exemptions only that portion of real property of such institution which is actually and regularly used for the purposes of the institution.

(b) The General Assembly may, by law:

(i) Establish standards and qualifications for private forest reserves, agricultural reserves, and land actively devoted to agricultural use, and make special provision for the taxation thereof;

(ii) Establish as a class or classes of subjects of taxation the property or privileges of persons who, because of age, disability, infirmity or poverty are determined to be in need of tax exemption or of special tax provisions, and for any such class or classes, uniform standards and qualifications. The Commonwealth, or any other taxing authority, may adopt or employ such class or classes and standards and qualifications, and except as herein provided may impose taxes, grant exemptions, or make special tax provisions in accordance therewith. No exemption or special provision shall be made under this clause with respect to taxes upon the sale or use of personal property, and no exemption from any tax upon real property shall be granted by the General Assembly under this clause unless the General Assembly shall provide for the reimbursement of local taxing authorities by or through the Commonwealth for revenue losses occasioned by such exemption;

(iii) Establish standards and qualifications by which local taxing authorities may make uniform special tax provisions applicable to a taxpayer for a limited period of time to encourage improvement of deteriorating property or areas by an individual, association or corporation, or to encourage industrial development by a non-profit corporation; and

(iv) Make special tax provisions on any increase in value of real estate resulting from residential construction. Such special tax provisions shall be applicable for a period not to exceed two years.

(v) Establish standards and qualifications by which local taxing authorities in counties of the first and second class may make uniform special real property tax provisions applicable to taxpayers who are longtime owner-occupants as shall be defined by the General Assembly of residences in areas where real property values have risen markedly as a consequence of the refurbishing or renovating of other deteriorating residences or the construction of new residences.

(vi) Authorize local taxing authorities to exclude from taxation an amount based on the assessed value of homestead property. The exclusions authorized by this clause shall not exceed 100% of the assessed value of each homestead property within a local taxing jurisdiction. A local taxing authority may not increase the millage rate of its tax on real property to pay for these exclusions.

(c) Citizens and residents of this Commonwealth, who served in any war or armed conflict in which the United States was engaged and were honorably discharged or released under honorable circumstances from active service, shall be exempt from the payment of all real property taxes upon the residence occupied by the said citizens and residents of this Commonwealth imposed by the Commonwealth of Pennsylvania or any of its political subdivisions if, as a result of military service, they are blind, paraplegic or double or quadruple amputees or have a service-connected disability declared by the United States Veterans Administration or its successor to be a total or 100% permanent disability, and if the State Veterans' Commission determines that such persons are in need of the tax exemptions granted herein. This exemption shall be extended to the unmarried surviving spouse upon the death of an eligible veteran provided that the State Veterans' Commission determines that such person is in need of the exemption.

SECTION 3. RECIPROCAL EXEMPTIONS. [119]

Taxation laws may grant exemptions or rebates to residents, or estates of residents, of other States which grant similar exemptions or rebates to residents, or estates of residents, of Pennsylvania.

SECTION 4. PUBLIC UTILITIES. [120]

The real property of public utilities is subject to real estate taxes imposed by local taxing authorities. Payment to the Commonwealth of gross receipts taxes or other special taxes in replacement of gross receipts taxes by a public utility and the distribution by the Commonwealth to the local taxing authorities of the amount as herein provided shall, however, be in lieu of local taxes upon its real property which is used or useful in furnishing its public utility service. The amount raised annually by such gross receipts or other special taxes shall not be less than the gross amount of real estate taxes which the local taxing authorities could have imposed upon such real property but for the exemption herein provided. This gross amount shall be determined in the manner provided by law. An amount equivalent to such real estate taxes shall be distributed annually among all local taxing authorities in the proportion which the total tax receipts of each local taxing authority bear to the total tax receipts of all local taxing authorities, or in such other equitable proportions as may be provided by law. Notwithstanding the provisions of this section, any law which presently subjects real property of public utilities to local real estate taxation by local taxing authorities shall remain in full force and effect.

SECTION 5. EXEMPTION FROM TAXATION RESTRICTED. [121]

All laws exempting property from taxation, other than the property above enumerated, shall be void.

SECTION 6. TAXATION OF CORPORATIONS. [122]

The power to tax corporations and corporate property shall not be surrendered or suspended by any contract or grant to which the Commonwealth shall be a party.

SECTION 7. COMMONWEALTH INDEBTEDNESS. [123]

(a) No debt shall be incurred by or on behalf of the Commonwealth except by law and in accordance with the provisions of this section.

(1) Debt may be incurred without limit to suppress insurrection, rehabilitate areas affected by man-made or natural disaster, or to implement unissued authority approved by the electors prior to the adoption of this article.

(2) The Governor, State Treasurer and Auditor General, acting jointly, may

(i) issue tax anticipation notes having a maturity within the fiscal year of issue and payable exclusively from revenues received in the same fiscal year, and

(ii) incur debt for the purpose of refunding other debt, if such refunding debt matures within the term of the original debt.

(3) Debt may be incurred without limit for purposes specifically itemized in the law authorizing such debt, if the question whether the debt shall be incurred has been submitted to the electors and approved by a majority of those voting on the question.

(4) Debt may be incurred without the approval of the electors for capital projects specifically itemized in a capital budget, if such debt will not cause the amount of all net debt outstanding to exceed one and three-quarters times the average of the annual tax revenues deposited in the previous five fiscal years as certified by the Auditor General. For the purposes of this subsection, debt outstanding shall not include debt incurred under clauses (1) and (2) (i), or debt incurred under clause (2) (ii) if the original debt would not be so

(2) considered, or debt incurred under subsection (3) unless the General Assembly shall so provide in the law authorizing such debt.

(b) All debt incurred for capital projects shall mature within a period not to exceed the estimated useful life of the projects as stated in the authorizing law, and when so stated shall be conclusive. All debt, except indebtedness permitted by clause (2) (i), shall be amortized in substantial and regular amounts, the first of which shall be due prior to the expiration of a period equal to one-tenth the term of the debt.

(c) As used in this section, debt shall mean the issued and outstanding obligations of the Commonwealth and shall include obligations of its agencies or authorities to the extent they are to be repaid from lease rentals or other charges payable directly or indirectly from revenues of the Commonwealth. Debt shall not include either (1) that portion of obligations to be repaid from charges made to the public for the use of the capital projects financed, as determined by the Auditor General, or (2) obligations to be repaid from lease rentals or other charges payable by a school district or other local taxing authority, or (3) obligations to be repaid by agencies or authorities created for the joint benefit of the Commonwealth and one or more other State governments.

(d) If sufficient funds are not appropriated for the timely payment of the interest upon and installments of principal of all debt, the State Treasurer shall set apart from the first revenues thereafter received applicable to the appropriate fund a sum sufficient to pay such interest and installments of principal, and shall so apply the money so set apart. The State Treasurer may be required to set aside and apply such revenues at the suit of any holder of Commonwealth obligations.

SECTION 8. COMMONWEALTH CREDIT NOT TO BE PLEDGED.[124]

The credit of the Commonwealth shall not be pledged or loaned to any individual, company, corporation or association nor shall the Commonwealth become a joint owner or stockholder in any company, corporation or association.

SECTION 9. MUNICIPAL DEBT NOT TO BE ASSUMED BY COMMONWEALTH. [125]

The Commonwealth shall not assume the debt, or any part thereof, of any county, city, borough, incorporated town, township or any similar general purpose unit of government unless such debt shall have been incurred to enable the Commonwealth to suppress insurrection or to assist the Commonwealth in the discharge of any portion of its present indebtedness.

SECTION 10. AUDIT. [126]

The financial affairs of any entity funded or financially aided by the Commonwealth, and all departments, boards, commissions, agencies, instrumentalities, authorities and institutions of the Commonwealth, shall be subject to audits made in accordance with generally accepted auditing standards. Any Commonwealth officer whose approval is necessary for any transaction relative to the financial affairs of the Commonwealth shall not be charged with the function of auditing that transaction after its occurrence.

SECTION 11. GASOLINE TAXES AND MOTOR LICENSE FEES RESTRICTED. [127]

(a) All proceeds from gasoline and other motor fuel excise taxes, motor vehicle registration fees and license taxes, operators' license fees and other excise taxes imposed on products used in motor transportation after providing therefrom for

(a) cost of administration and collection,

(b) payment of obligations incurred in the construction and reconstruction of public highways and bridges shall be appropriated by the General Assembly to agencies of the State or political subdivisions thereof; and used solely for construction, reconstruction, maintenance and repair of and safety on public highways and bridges and costs and expenses incident thereto, and for the payment of obligations incurred for such purposes, and shall not be diverted by transfer or otherwise to any other purpose, except that loans may be made by the State from the proceeds of such taxes and fees for a single period not exceeding eight months, but no such loan shall be made within the period of one year from any preceding loan, and every loan made in any fiscal year shall be repayable within one month after the beginning of the next fiscal year.

(b) All proceeds from aviation fuel excise taxes, after providing therefrom for the cost of administration and collection, shall be appropriated by the General Assembly to agencies of the State or political subdivisions thereof and used solely for: the purchase, construction, reconstruction, operation and maintenance of airports and other air navigation facilities; aircraft accident investigation; the operation, maintenance and other costs of aircraft owned or leased by the Commonwealth; any other purpose reasonably related to air navigation including but not limited to the reimbursement of airport property owners for property tax expenditures; and costs and expenses incident thereto and for the payment of obligations incurred for such purposes, and shall not be diverted by transfer or otherwise to any other purpose.

SECTION 12. GOVERNOR'S BUDGETS AND FINANCIAL PLAN. [128]

Annually, at the times set by law, the Governor shall submit to the General Assembly:

(a) A balanced operating budget for the ensuing fiscal year setting forth in detail

(i) proposed expenditures classified by department or agency and by program and

(ii) estimated revenues from all sources. If estimated revenues and available surplus are less than proposed expenditures, the Governor shall recommend specific additional sources of revenue sufficient to pay the deficiency and the estimated revenue to be derived from each source;

(b) A capital budget for the ensuing fiscal year setting forth in detail proposed expenditures to be financed from the proceeds of obligations of the Commonwealth or of its agencies or authorities or from operating funds; and

(c) A financial plan for not less than the next succeeding five fiscal years, which plan shall include for each such fiscal year:

(i) Projected operating expenditures classified by department or agency and by program, in reasonable detail, and estimated revenues, by major categories, from existing and additional sources, and

(ii) Projected expenditures for capital projects specifically itemized by purpose, and the proposed sources of financing each.

SECTION 13. APPROPRIATIONS. [129]

(a) Operating budget appropriations made by the General Assembly shall not exceed the actual and estimated revenues and surplus available in the same fiscal year.

(b) The General Assembly shall adopt a capital budget for the ensuing fiscal year.

SECTION 14. SURPLUS. [130]

All surplus of operating funds at the end of the fiscal year shall be appropriated during the ensuing fiscal year by the General Assembly.

SECTION 15. PROJECT "70". [131]

In addition to the purposes stated in Article VIII, section 7 of this Constitution, the Commonwealth may be authorized by law to create debt and to issue bonds to the amount of $70,000,000 for the acquisition of land for State parks, reservoirs and other conservation and recreation and historical preservation purposes, and for participation by the Commonwealth with political subdivisions in the acquisition of land for parks, reservoirs and other conservation and recreation and historical preservation purposes, subject to such conditions and limitations as the General Assembly may prescribe.

SECTION 16. LAND AND WATER CONSERVATION AND RECLAMATION FUND. [132]

In addition to the purposes stated in Article VIII, Section 7 of this Constitution, the Commonwealth may be authorized by law to create a debt and issue bonds in the amount of $500,000,000 for a Land and Water Conservation and Reclamation Fund to be used for the conservation and reclamation of land and water resources of the Commonwealth, including the elimination of acid mine drainage, sewage, and other pollution from the streams of the Commonwealth, the provision of State financial assistance to political subdivisions and municipal authorities of the Commonwealth of Pennsylvania for the construction of sewage treatment plants, the restoration of abandoned strip-mined areas, the control and extinguishment of surface and underground mine fires, the alleviation and prevention of subsidence resulting from mining operations, and the acquisition of additional lands and the reclamation and development of park and recreational lands acquired pursuant to the authority of Article VIII, Section 15 of this Constitution, subject to such conditions and liabilities as the General Assembly may prescribe.

SECTION 17. SPECIAL EMERGENCY LEGISLATION. [133]

(a) Notwithstanding any provisions of this Constitution to the contrary, the General Assembly shall have the authority to enact laws providing for tax rebates, credits, exemptions, grants-in-aid, State supplementations, or otherwise provide special provisions for individuals, corporations, associations or nonprofit institutions, including nonpublic schools (whether sectarian or nonsectarian) in order to alleviate the danger, damage, suffering or hardship faced by such individuals, corporations, associations, institutions or nonpublic schools as a result of Great Storms or Floods of September 1971, of June 1972, or of 1974, or of 1975 or of 1976.

(b) Notwithstanding the provisions of Article III, section 29 subsequent to a Presidential declaration of an emergency or of a major disaster in any part of this Commonwealth, the General Assembly shall have the authority by a vote of two-thirds of all members elected to each House to make appropriations limited to moneys required for Federal emergency or major disaster relief. This subsection may retroactively to any Presidential declaration or of a major disaster in 1976 or 1977.

ARTICLE IX
LOCAL GOVERNMENT [134]

SECTION 1. LOCAL GOVERNMENT. [135]

The General Assembly shall provide by general law for local government within the Commonwealth. Such general law shall be uniform as to all classes of local government regarding procedural matters.

SECTION 2. HOME RULE. [136]

Municipalities shall have the right and power to frame and adopt home rule charters. Adoption, amendment or repeal of a home rule charter shall be by referendum. The General Assembly shall provide the procedure by which a home rule charter may be framed and its adoption, amendment or repeal presented to the electors. If the General Assembly does not so provide, a home rule charter or a procedure for framing and presenting a home rule charter may be presented to the electors by initiative or by the governing body of the municipality. A municipality which has a home rule charter may exercise any power or perform any function not denied by this Constitution, by its home rule charter or by the General Assembly at any time.

SECTION 3. OPTIONAL PLANS.

Municipalities shall have the right and power to adopt optional forms of government as provided by law. The General Assembly shall provide optional forms of government for all municipalities. An optional form of government shall be presented to the electors by initiative, by the governing body of the municipality, or by the General Assembly. Adoption or repeal of an optional form of government shall be by referendum.

SECTION 4. COUNTY GOVERNMENT.

County officers shall consist of commissioners, controllers or auditors, district attorneys, public defenders, treasurers, sheriffs, registers of wills, recorders of deeds, prothonotaries, clerks of the courts, and such others as may from time to time be provided by law. County officers, except for public defenders who shall be appointed as shall be provided by law, shall be elected at the municipal elections and shall hold their offices for the term of four years, beginning on the first Monday of January next after their election, and until their successors shall be duly qualified; all vacancies shall be filled in such a manner as may be provided by law.

County officers shall be paid only by salary as provided by law for services performed for the county or any other governmental unit. Fees incidental to the conduct of any county office shall be payable directly to the county or the Commonwealth, or as otherwise provided by law.

Three county commissioners shall be elected in each county. In the election of these officers each qualified elector shall vote for no more than two persons, and the three persons receiving the highest number of votes shall be elected. Provisions for county government in this section shall apply to every county except a county which has adopted a home rule charter or an optional form of government. One of the optional forms of county government provided by law shall include the provisions of this section.

SECTION 5. INTERGOVERNMENTAL COOPERATION.

A municipality by act of its governing body may, or upon being required by initiative and referendum in the area affected shall, cooperate or agree in the exercise of any function, power or responsibility with, or delegate or transfer any function, power or responsibility to, one or more other governmental units including other municipalities or districts, the Federal government, any other state or its governmental units, or any newly created governmental unit.

SECTION 6. AREA GOVERNMENT.

The General Assembly shall provide for the establishment and dissolution of government of areas involving two or more municipalities or parts thereof.

SECTION 7. AREA-WIDE POWERS.

The General Assembly may grant powers to area governments or to municipalities within a given geographical area in which there exists intergovernmental cooperation or area government and designate the classes of municipalities subject to such legislation.

SECTION 8. CONSOLIDATION, MERGER OR BOUNDARY CHANGE. [137]

Uniform Legislation.--The General Assembly shall, within two (2) years following the adoption of this article, enact uniform legislation establishing the procedure for consolidation, merger or change of the boundaries of municipalities.

Initiative.--The electors of any municipality shall have the right, by initiative and referendum, to consolidate, merge and change boundaries by a majority vote of those voting thereon in each municipality, without the approval of any governing body.

Study.--The General Assembly shall designate an agency of the Commonwealth to study consolidation, merger and boundary changes, advise municipalities on all problems which might be connected therewith, and initiate local referendum.

Legislative Power.--Nothing herein shall prohibit or prevent the General Assembly from providing additional methods for consolidation, merger or change of boundaries.

SECTION 9. APPROPRIATION FOR PUBLIC PURPOSES.

The General Assembly shall not authorize any municipality or incorporated district to become a stockholder in any company, association or corporation, or to obtain or appropriate money for, or to loan its credit to, any corporation, association, institution or individual. The General Assembly may provide standards by which municipalities or school districts may give financial assistance or lease property to public service, industrial or commercial enterprises if it shall find that such assistance or leasing is necessary to the health, safety or welfare of the Commonwealth or any municipality or school district. Existing authority of any municipality or incorporated district to obtain or appropriate money for, or to loan its credit to, any corporation, association, institution or individual, is preserved.

SECTION 10. LOCAL GOVERNMENT DEBT.

Subject only to the restrictions imposed by this section, the General Assembly shall prescribe the debt limits of all units of local government including municipalities and school districts. For such purposes, the debt limit base shall be a percentage of the total revenue, as defined by the General Assembly, of the unit of local government computed over a specific period immediately preceding the year of borrowing. The debt limit to be prescribed in every such case shall exclude all indebtedness **(1)** for any project to the extent that it is self-liquidating or self-supporting or which has heretofore been defined as self-liquidating or self-supporting, or **(2)** which has been approved by referendum held in such manner as shall be provided by law. The provisions of this paragraph shall not apply to the City or County of Philadelphia. Any unit of local government, including municipalities and school districts, incurring any indebtedness, shall at or before the time of so doing adopt a covenant, which shall be binding upon it so long as any such indebtedness shall remain unpaid, to make payments out of its sinking fund or any other of its revenues or funds at such time and in such annual amounts specified in such covenant as shall be sufficient for the payment of the interest thereon and the principal thereof when due.

SECTION 11. LOCAL REAPPORTIONMENT.
Within the year following that in which the Federal decennial census is officially reported as required by Federal law, and at such other times as the governing body of any municipality shall deem necessary, each municipality having a governing body not entirely elected at large shall be reapportioned, by its governing body or as shall otherwise be provided by uniform law, into districts which shall be composed of compact and contiguous territory as nearly equal in population as practicable, for the purpose of describing the districts for those not elected at large.

SECTION 12. PHILADELPHIA DEBT.
The debt of the City of Philadelphia may be increased in such amount that the total debt of said city shall not exceed 13 1/2% of the average of the annual assessed valuations of the taxable realty therein, during the ten years immediately preceding the year in which such increase is made, but said city shall not increase its indebtedness to an amount exceeding 3% upon such average assessed valuation of realty, without the consent of the electors thereof at a public election held in such manner as shall be provided by law. In ascertaining the debt-incurring capacity of the City of Philadelphia at any time, there shall be deducted from the debt of said city so much of such debt as shall have been incurred, or is about to be incurred, and the proceeds thereof expended, or about to be expended, upon any public improvement, or in construction, purchase or condemnation of any

public utility, or part thereof, or facility therefor, if such public improvement or public utility, or part thereof, or facility therefor, whether separately, or in connection with any other public improvement or public utility, or part thereof, or facility therefor, may reasonably be expected to yield revenue in excess of operating expenses sufficient to pay the interest and sinking fund charges thereon. The method of determining such amount, so to be deducted, shall be as now prescribed, or which may hereafter be prescribed by law. In incurring indebtedness for any purpose the City of Philadelphia may issue its obligations maturing not later than 50 years from the date thereof, with provision for a sinking fund to be in equal or graded annual or other periodical installments. Where any indebtedness shall be or shall have been incurred by said City of Philadelphia for the purpose of the construction or improvement of public works or utilities of any character, from which income or revenue is to be derived by said city, or for the reclamation of land to be used in the construction of wharves or docks owned or to be owned by said city, such obligations may be in an amount sufficient to provide for, and may include the amount of the interest and sinking fund charges accruing and which may accrue thereon throughout the period of construction, and until the expiration of one year after the completion of the work for which said indebtedness shall have been incurred. No debt shall be incurred by, or on behalf of, the County of Philadelphia.

SECTION 13. ABOLITION OF COUNTY OFFICES IN PHILADELPHIA.

(a) In Philadelphia all county offices are hereby abolished, and the city shall henceforth perform all functions of county government within its area through officers selected in such manner as may be provided by law.

(b) Local and special laws, regulating the affairs of the City of Philadelphia and creating offices or prescribing the powers and duties of officers of the City of Philadelphia, shall be valid notwithstanding the provisions of section 32 of Article III of this Constitution.

(c) All laws applicable to the County of Philadelphia shall apply to the City of Philadelphia.

(d) The City of Philadelphia shall have, assume and take over all powers, property, obligations and indebtedness of the County of Philadelphia.

(e) The provisions of section 2 of this article shall apply with full force and effect to the functions of the county government hereafter to be performed by the city government.

(f) Upon adoption of this amendment all county officers shall become officers of the City of Philadelphia, and until the General Assembly shall otherwise provide, shall continue to perform their duties and be elected, appointed, compensated and organized in such manner as may be provided by the provisions of this Constitution and the laws of the Commonwealth in effect at the time this amendment becomes effective, but such officers serving when this amendment becomes effective shall be permitted to complete their terms.

SECTION 14. DEFINITIONS.

As used in this article, the following words shall have the following meanings:

"Municipality" means a county, city, borough, incorporated town, township or any similar general purpose unit of government which shall hereafter be created by the General Assembly.

"Initiative" means the filing with the applicable election officials at least 90 days prior to the next primary or general election of a petition containing a proposal for referendum signed by electors comprising 5% of the number of electors voting for the office of Governor in the last gubernatorial general election in each municipality or area affected. The applicable election official shall place the proposal on the ballot in a manner fairly representing the content of the petition for decision by referendum at said election. Initiative on a similar question shall not be submitted more often than once in five years. No enabling law shall be required for initiative. "Referendum" means approval of a question placed on the ballot, by initiative or otherwise, by a majority vote of the electors voting thereon.

ARTICLE X
PRIVATE CORPORATIONS [138]

SECTION 1. CERTAIN UNUSED CHARTERS VOID.

The charters and privileges granted prior to 1874 to private corporations which had not been organized in good faith and commenced business prior to 1874 shall be void.

SECTION 2. CERTAIN CHARTERS TO BE SUBJECT TO THE CONSTITUTION.

Private corporations which have accepted or accept the Constitution of this Commonwealth or the benefits of any law passed by the General Assembly after 1873 governing the affairs of corporations shall hold their charters subject to the provisions of the Constitution of this Commonwealth.

SECTION 3. REVOCATION, AMENDMENT AND REPEAL OF CHARTERS AND CORPORATION LAWS.

All charters of private corporations and all present and future common or statutory law with respect to the formation or regulation of private corporations or prescribing powers, rights, duties or liabilities of private corporations or their officers, directors or shareholders may be revoked, amended or repealed.

SECTION 4. COMPENSATION FOR PROPERTY TAKEN BY CORPORATIONS UNDER RIGHT OF EMINENT DOMAIN.

Municipal and other corporations invested with the privilege of taking private property for public use shall make just compensation for property taken, injured or destroyed by the construction or enlargement of their works, highways or improvements and compensation shall be paid or secured before the taking, injury or destruction.

ARTICLE XI
AMENDMENTS [139]

Section
1. Proposal of amendments by the General Assembly and their adoption.

SECTION 1. PROPOSAL OF AMENDMENTS BY THE GENERAL ASSEMBLY AND THEIR ADOPTION. [140]

Amendments to this Constitution may be proposed in the Senate or House of Representatives; and if the same shall be agreed to by a majority of the members elected to each House, such proposed amendment or amendments shall be entered on their journals with the yeas and nays taken thereon, and the Secretary of the Commonwealth shall cause the same to be published three months before the next general election, in at least two (2) newspapers in every county in which such newspapers shall be published; and if, in the General Assembly next afterwards chosen, such proposed amendment or amendments shall be agreed to by a majority of the members elected to each House, the Secretary of the Commonwealth shall cause the same again to be published in the manner aforesaid; and such proposed amendment or amendments shall be submitted to the qualified electors of the State in such manner, and at such time at least three months after being so agreed to by the two (2) Houses, as the General Assembly shall prescribe; and, if such amendment or amendments shall be approved by a majority of those voting thereon, such amendment or amendments shall become a part of the Constitution; but no amendment or amendments shall be submitted oftener than once in five (5) years.

When two (2) or more amendments shall be submitted they shall be voted upon separately.

(a) In the event a major emergency threatens or is about to threaten the Commonwealth and if the safety or welfare of the Commonwealth requires prompt amendment of this Constitution, such amendments to this Constitution may be proposed in the Senate or House of Representatives at any regular or special session of the General Assembly, and if agreed to by at least two-thirds (2/3) of the members elected to each House, a proposed amendment shall be entered on the journal of each House with the yeas and nays taken thereon and the official in charge of statewide elections shall promptly publish such proposed amendment in at least two newspapers in every county in which such newspapers are published. Such amendment shall then be submitted to the qualified electors of the Commonwealth in such manner, and at such time, at least one month after being agreed to by both Houses as the General Assembly prescribes.

(b) If an emergency amendment is approved by a majority of the qualified electors voting thereon, it shall become part of this Constitution. When two (2) or more emergency amendments are submitted they shall be voted on separately.

SCHEDULES TO CONSTITUTION OF PENNSYLVANIA

SCHEDULE NO. 1 (ADOPTED WITH THE CONSTITUTION) [141]

That no inconvenience may arise from the changes in the Constitution of the Commonwealth, and in order to carry the same into complete operation, it is hereby declared, that:

SECTION 1. WHEN TO TAKE EFFECT.
This Constitution shall take effect on the first day of January, in the year one thousand eight hundred and seventy-four (1874), for all purposes not otherwise provided for therein.

SECTION 2. FORMER LAWS REMAIN IN FORCE.
All laws in force in this Commonwealth at the time of the adoption of this Constitution not inconsistent therewith, and all rights, actions, prosecutions and contracts shall continue as if this Constitution had not been adopted.

SECTION 3. ELECTION OF SENATORS.
At the general election in the years one thousand eight hundred and seventy-four (1874) and one thousand eight hundred and seventy-five (1875), Senators shall be elected in all districts where there shall be vacancies. Those elected in the year one thousand eight hundred and seventy-four (1874) shall serve for two (2) years, and those elected in the year one thousand eight hundred and seventy-five (1875) shall serve for one (1) year. Senators now elected and those whose terms are unexpired shall

represent the districts in which they reside until the end of the terms for which they were elected.

SECTION 4. ELECTION OF SENATORS (CONTINUED).

At the general election in the year one thousand eight hundred and seventy-six (1876), Senators shall be elected from even-numbered districts to serve for two (2) years, and from odd-numbered districts to serve for four (4) years.

SECTION 5. ELECTION OF GOVERNOR.

The first election of Governor under this Constitution shall be at the general election in the year one thousand eight hundred and seventy-five (1875), when a Governor shall be elected for three (3) years; and the term of the Governor elected in the year one thousand eight hundred and seventy-eight (1878) and of those thereafter elected shall be for four (4) years, according to the provisions of this Constitution.

SECTION 6. ELECTION OF LIEUTENANT GOVERNOR.

At the general election in the year one thousand eight hundred and seventy-four (1874), a Lieutenant Governor shall be elected according to the provisions of this Constitution.

SECTION 7. SECRETARY OF INTERNAL AFFAIRS.

The Secretary of Internal Affairs shall be elected at the first general election after the adoption of this Constitution; and, when the said officer shall be duly elected and qualified, the office of Surveyor General shall be abolished. The Surveyor General in office at the time of the adoption of this Constitution shall continue in office until the expiration of the term for which he was elected.

SECTION 8. SUPERINTENDENT OF PUBLIC INSTRUCTION.

When the Superintendent of Public Instruction shall be duly qualified the office of Superintendent of Common Schools shall cease.

SECTION 9. ELIGIBILITY OF PRESENT OFFICERS.

Nothing contained in this Constitution shall be construed to render any person now holding any State office for a first official term ineligible for re-election at the end of such term.

SECTION 10. JUDGES OF SUPREME COURT.

The judges of the Supreme Court in office when this Constitution shall take effect shall continue until their commissions severally expire. Two (2) judges in addition to the number now composing the said court shall be elected at the first general election after the adoption of this Constitution.

SECTION 11. COURTS OF RECORD.

All courts of record and all existing courts which are not specified in this Constitution shall continue in existence until the first day of December, in the year one thousand eight hundred and seventy-five, without abridgment of their present jurisdiction, but no longer. The court of first criminal jurisdiction for the counties of Schuylkill, Lebanon and Dauphin is hereby abolished, and all causes and proceedings pending therein in the county of Schuylkill shall be tried and disposed of in the courts of *oyer* and *terminer* and quarter sessions of the peace of said county.

SECTION 12. REGISTER'S COURTS ABOLISHED.
The register's courts now in existence shall be abolished on the first day of January next succeeding the adoption of this Constitution.

SECTION 13. JUDICIAL DISTRICTS.
The General Assembly shall, at the next session after the adoption of this Constitution, designate the several judicial districts as required by this Constitution. The judges in commission when such designation shall be made shall continue during their unexpired terms judges of the new districts in which they reside; but, when there shall be two (2) judges residing in the same district, the president judge shall elect to which district he shall be assigned, and the additional law judge shall be assigned to the other district.

SECTION 14. DECENNIAL ADJUSTMENT OF JUDICIAL DISTRICTS.
The General Assembly shall, at the next succeeding session after each decennial census and not oftener, designate the several judicial districts as required by this Constitution.

SECTION 15. JUDGES IN COMMISSION.
Judges learned in the law of any court of record holding commissions in force at the adoption of this

Constitution shall hold their respective offices until the expiration of the terms for which they were commissioned, and until their successors shall be duly qualified. The Governor shall commission the president judge of the court of first criminal jurisdiction for the counties of Schuylkill, Lebanon and Dauphin as a judge of the court of common pleas of Schuylkill county, for the unexpired term of his office.

SECTION 16. PRESIDENT JUDGES; CASTING LOTS; ASSOCIATE JUDGES.

After the expiration of the term of any president judge of any court of common pleas, in commission at the adoption of this Constitution, the judge of such court learned in the law and oldest in commission shall be the president judge thereof; and when two or more judges are elected at the same time in any judicial district they shall decide by lot which shall be president judge; but when the president judge of a court shall be re-elected he shall continue to be president judge of that court. Associate judges not learned in the law, elected after the adoption of this Constitution, shall be commissioned to hold their offices for the term of five (5) years from the first day of January next after their election.

SECTION 17. COMPENSATION OF JUDGES.

The General Assembly, at the first session after the adoption of this Constitution, shall fix and determine the compensation of the judges of the Supreme Court and of the judges of the several judicial districts of the Commonwealth; and the provisions of the fifteenth section of the article on Legislation shall not be deemed inconsistent herewith. Nothing contained in this Constitution shall be held to reduce the compensation now paid to any law judge of this Commonwealth now in commission.

SECTION 18. COURTS OF PHILADELPHIA AND ALLEGHENY COUNTIES; ORGANIZATION IN PHILADELPHIA.

The courts of common pleas in the counties of Philadelphia and Allegheny shall be composed of the present judges of the district court and court of common pleas of said counties until their offices shall severally end, and of such other judges as may from time to time be selected. For the purpose of first organization in Philadelphia the judges of the court number one (1) shall be Judges Allison, Pierce and Paxson; of the court number two (2), Judges Hare, Mitchell and one (1) other judge to be elected; of the court number three (3), Judges Ludlow, Finletter and Lynd; and of the court number four, Judges Thayer, Briggs and one other judge to be elected. The judge first named shall be the president judge of said courts respectively, and thereafter the president judge shall be the judge oldest in commission; but any president judge, re-elected in the same court or district, shall continue to be president judge thereof. The additional judges for courts numbers two (2) and four (4) shall be voted for and elected at the first general election after the adoption of this Constitution, in the same manner as the two (2) additional judges of the Supreme Court, and they shall decide by lot to which court they shall belong. Their term of office shall commence on the first Monday of January, in the year one thousand eight hundred and seventy-five (1875).

SECTION 19. ORGANIZATION OF COURTS IN ALLEGHENY COUNTY.

In the county of Allegheny, for the purpose of first organization under this Constitution, the judges of the court of common pleas, at the time of the adoption of this Constitution, shall be the judges of the court number one, and the judges of the district court, at the same date, shall be the judges of the common pleas number two. The president judges of the common pleas and district court shall be president judge of said courts number one and two, respectively, until their offices shall end; and thereafter the judge oldest in commission shall be president judge; but any president judge re-elected in the same court, or district, shall continue to be president judge thereof.

SECTION 20. WHEN RE-ORGANIZATION OF COURTS TO TAKE EFFECT.

The organization of the courts of common pleas under this Constitution for the counties of Philadelphia and Allegheny shall take effect on the first Monday of January, one thousand eight hundred and seventy-five (1875), and existing courts in said counties shall continue with their present powers and jurisdiction until that date, but no new suits shall be instituted in the courts of *nisi prius* after the adoption of this Constitution.

SECTION 21. CAUSES PENDING IN PHILADELPHIA; TRANSFER OF RECORDS.

The causes and proceedings pending in the court of *nisi prius*, court of common pleas, and district court in Philadelphia shall be tried and disposed of in the court of common pleas. The records and dockets of said courts shall be transferred to the prothonotary's office of said county.

SECTION 22. CAUSES PENDING IN ALLEGHENY COUNTY.

The causes and proceedings pending in the court of common pleas in the county of Allegheny shall be tried and disposed of in the court number one; and the causes and proceedings pending in the district court shall be tried and disposed of in the court number two (2).

SECTION 23. PROTHONOTARY OF PHILADELPHIA COUNTY.

The prothonotary of the court of common pleas of Philadelphia shall be first appointed by the judges of said court on the first Monday of December, in the year one thousand eight hundred and seventy-five (1875), and the present prothonotary of the district court in said county shall be the prothonotary of the said court of common pleas until said date when his commission shall expire, and the present clerk of the court of *oyer* and *terminer* and quarter sessions of the peace in Philadelphia shall be the clerk of such court until the expiration of his present commission on the first Monday of December, in the year one thousand eight hundred and seventy-five (1875).

SECTION 24. ALDERMEN.

In cities containing over fifty thousand inhabitants, except Philadelphia, all aldermen in office at the time of the adoption of this Constitution shall continue in office until the expiration of their commissions, and at the election for city and ward officers in the year one thousand eight hundred and seventy-five(1875) one (1) alderman shall be elected in each ward as provided in this Constitution.

SECTION 25. MAGISTRATES IN PHILADELPHIA.

In Philadelphia magistrates in lieu of aldermen shall be chosen, as required in this Constitution, at the election in said city for city and ward officers in the year one thousand eight hundred and seventy-five (1875); their term of office shall commence on the first Monday of April succeeding their election. The terms of office of aldermen in said city holding or entitled to commissions at the time of the adoption of this Constitution shall not be affected thereby.

SECTION 26. TERM OF PRESENT OFFICERS.

All persons in office in this Commonwealth at the time of the adoption of this Constitution, and at the first election under it, shall hold their respective offices until the term for which they have been elected or appointed shall expire, and until their successors shall be duly qualified, unless otherwise provided in this Constitution.

SECTION 27. OATH OF OFFICE.

The seventh article of this Constitution prescribing an oath of office shall take effect on and after the first day of January, one thousand eight hundred and seventy-five (1875).

SECTION 28. COUNTY COMMISSIONERS AND AUDITORS.

The terms of office of county commissioners and county auditors, chosen prior to the year one thousand eight hundred and seventy-five (1875), which shall not have expired before the first Monday of January in the year one thousand eight hundred and seventy-six (1876), shall expire on that day.

SECTION 29. COMPENSATION OF PRESENT OFFICERS.

All State, county, city, ward, borough and township officers in office at the time of the adoption of this Constitution, whose compensation is not provided for by salaries alone, shall continue to receive the compensation allowed them by law until the expiration of their respective terms of office.

SECTION 30. RENEWAL OF OATH OF OFFICE.

All State and judicial officers heretofore elected, sworn, affirmed, or in office when this Constitution shall take effect, shall severally, within one (1) month after such adoption, take and subscribe an oath, or affirmation, to support this Constitution.

SECTION 31. ENFORCING LEGISLATION.

The General Assembly at its first session, or as soon as may be after the adoption of this Constitution, shall pass such laws as may be necessary to carry the same into full force and effect.

SECTION 32. AN ORDINANCE DECLARED VALID.

The ordinance passed by this Convention, entitled "An ordinance for submitting the amended Constitution of Pennsylvania to a vote of the electors thereof," shall be held to be valid for all the purposes thereof.

SECTION 33. CITY COMMISSIONERS OF PHILADELPHIA.

The words "county commissioners," wherever used in this Constitution and in any ordinance accompanying the same, shall be held to include the commissioners for the city of Philadelphia.

SCHEDULE NO. 2
(AMENDMENTS OF NOVEMBER 2, 1909) [142]

SECTION 1. ADJUSTMENTS OF TERMS OF PUBLIC OFFICERS.

That no inconvenience may arise from the changes in the Constitution of the Commonwealth, and in order to carry the same into complete operation, it is hereby declared that--

In the case of officers elected by the people, all terms of office fixed by act of Assembly at an odd number of years shall each be lengthened one (1) year, but the Legislature may change the length of the term, provided the terms for which such officers are elected shall always be for an even number of years. The above extension of official terms shall not affect officers elected at the general election of one thousand nine hundred and eight (1908); nor any city, ward, borough, township, or election division officers, whose terms of office, under existing law, end in the year one thousand nine hundred and ten (1910). In the year one thousand nine hundred and ten (1910) the municipal election shall be held on the third Tuesday of February as heretofore; but all officers chosen at that election to an office the regular term of which is two (2) years, and also all election officers and assessors chosen at that election, shall serve until the first Monday of December in the year one thousand nine hundred and eleven. All officers chosen at that election to offices the term of which is now four years, or is made four years by the operation of these amendments or this schedule, shall serve until the first Monday of December in the year one thousand nine hundred and thirteen (1913). All justices of the peace, magistrates, and aldermen, chosen at that election, shall serve until the first Monday of December in the year one thousand nine hundred and fifteen (1915). After the year nineteen hundred and ten (1910), and until the Legislature shall otherwise provide, all terms of city, ward, borough, township, and election division officers shall begin on the first Monday of December in an odd-numbered year.   All city, ward, borough, and township officers holding office at the date of the approval of these amendments, whose terms of office may end in the year one thousand nine hundred and eleven (1911), shall continue to hold their offices until the first Monday of December of that year.   All judges of the courts for the several judicial districts, and also all county officers, holding office at the date of the approval of these amendments, whose terms of office may end in the year one thousand nine hundred and eleven (1911), shall continue to hold their offices until the first Monday of January, one thousand nine hundred and twelve (1912).

APPENDIX TO
CONSTITUTION OF PENNSYLVANIA

Supplementary Provisions of Constitutional
Amendments
— — —

1967, MAY 16, P.L.1044, J.R.4
Schedule. Terms of State Treasurer and Auditor General. That no inconvenience may arise from changes in Article IV of the Constitution of this Commonwealth, it is hereby declared that the State Treasurer and Auditor General first elected after this amended article becomes effective shall serve terms beginning the first Tuesday in May next following their election and expiring four years from the third Tuesday in January next ensuing their election. [143]

1968, APRIL 23, P.L.APP.3, PROP. NO.1
Schedule. Effective date of amendment.
The foregoing amendment to Article II of the Constitution of Pennsylvania if approved by the electorate voting on April 23, 1968, shall become effective the year following that in which the next Federal decennial census is officially reported as required by Federal law. 144

1968, APRIL 23, P.L.APP.3, PROP. NO.2
Schedule. Effective date of amendment.
The foregoing amendment to Article II of the Constitution
of Pennsylvania if approved by the electorate voting on April 23, 1968, shall become effective the year following that in which the next Federal decennial census is officially reported as required by Federal law. [145]

1968, APRIL 23, P.L.APP.5, PROP. NO.3
SECTION 4. REPEALS.
Effective when the last bonds have been issued under their authority, sections 24 and 25 of Article VIII of the Constitution of Pennsylvania are hereby repealed. [146]

1968, APRIL 23, P.L.APP.7, PROP. NO.4
SECTION 3. EFFECTIVE DATE OF AMENDMENTS.
The following schedule is adopted: Sections 10, 12, 13 and 14 of Article VIII shall take effect as soon as possible, but no later than July 1, 1970.

1968, APRIL 23, P.L.APP.9, PROP. NO.5
SECTION 4. EFFECTIVE DATE OF AMENDMENTS.
Sections 1 and 2 shall take effect as soon as possible, but no later than July 1, 1970. Section 4 shall take effect July 1, 1970, unless the General Assembly earlier provides enabling legislation in accordance therewith.

1968, APRIL 23, P.L.APP.11, PROP. NO.6
SECTION 3. EFFECTIVE DATE AND INTERPRETATION OF AMENDMENTS.
This new article and the repeal of existing sections shall take effect on the date of approval by the electorate, except that the following sections shall take effect on the effective date of legislation adopted pursuant to the sections or the date indicated below, whichever shall first occur. The first, third and fourth paragraphs of section 8 shall take effect two years after the effective date. The second sentence of section 1, the fourth sentence of section 2, all of section 3, the third paragraph of section 4, and the first paragraph of section 10 shall take effect four years after the effective date. The second sentence of section 1 and the first paragraph of section 8 on Uniform Legislation shall be construed

so as to be consistent with the jurisdiction of this Convention. [148]

1968, APRIL 23, P.L.APP.16, PROP. NO.7
SECTION 2. REPEALS.
Article V of the Constitution of Pennsylvania is repealed in its entirety, and those provisions of Schedules No. 1 and No. 2 are repealed to the extent they are inconsistent with this article and attached schedule. [149]

1972, NOVEMBER 7, 1ST SP.SESS., P.L.1970, J.R.1
SECTION 1. PREAMBLE.
Millions of Pennsylvanians have suffered greatly from the ravages of the most disastrous flood in the history of the Commonwealth. This flood has left devastation in its wake. Thousands of people have been left homeless and countless industrial and commercial establishments and public facilities have been damaged or destroyed. It is imperative that the victims of this disaster immediately receive the fullest possible aid from both the public and private sectors in order to clean up and rebuild the affected areas of the Commonwealth. In addition, many Pennsylvanians suffered greatly as a result of the Great Storm or Flood of September, 1971.

The General Assembly desires to alleviate such storm or economic deprivation caused by the flood, but is limited in its efforts by rigid restrictions in the Constitution of the Commonwealth of Pennsylvania. The safety and welfare of the Commonwealth requires prompt amendment to the Constitution of the Commonwealth of Pennsylvania. The following amendment to the Constitution of the Commonwealth of Pennsylvania is proposed in accordance with the emergency provisions contained in subsections (a) and (b) of section one of the eleventh article thereof:

That article eight of the Constitution of the Commonwealth of Pennsylvania be amended by adding a new section to read:

1975, NOVEMBER 4, P.L.622, J.R.2
SECTION 1. PREAMBLE.

Many Pennsylvanians have suffered greatly from the ravages of great storms or floods in the last few years. The great storms or floods of 1974 and 1975 are additional major disasters causing loss of life and great damage and destruction to property of individuals, industrial and commercial establishments and public facilities. It is imperative that the victims of these disasters immediately receive the fullest possible aid from both the public and private sectors in order to clean up and rebuild the affected areas of the Commonwealth and that persons in the Commonwealth be eligible for the maximum available aid from the government of the United States. The General Assembly desires to alleviate such storm or economic deprivation caused by the floods but is limited in its efforts by rigid restrictions in the Constitution of the Commonwealth of Pennsylvania. The safety and welfare of the Commonwealth requires prompt amendment to the Constitution of the Commonwealth of Pennsylvania. The following amendment to the Constitution of the Commonwealth of Pennsylvania is proposed in accordance with the emergency provisions contained in subsections (a) and (b) of section one of the eleventh article thereof: That section seventeen (17) of article eight (8) of the Constitution of the Commonwealth of Pennsylvania be amended to read: ***

1977, NOVEMBER 8, P.L.362, J.R.2

SECTION 1. PREAMBLE.

Many Pennsylvanians have suffered greatly from the ravages of Great Storms and Floods in recent years. The Great Storms or Floods of 1974, 1975, 1976 and 1977 were additional major disasters causing loss of life and great damage and destruction to property of individuals, industrial and commercial establishments and public facilities. It is imperative that the victims of these disasters receive the fullest possible aid from both the Federal Government and the Commonwealth in order to accomplish a speedy recovery. The Congress of the United States, through enactment of the Disaster Relief Act of 1974, Public Law 93-288, has authorized the making of certain disaster relief grants. The General Assembly wishes to make such Federal disaster relief grants, or other grants made available from Federal programs hereafter enacted, available to eligible individuals and families in order to alleviate the deprivation caused by storms or floods which have occurred in the past and seeks to address those emergencies of future years. However, the General Assembly is limited by rigid restrictions in the Constitution of the Commonwealth of Pennsylvania. The safety and welfare of the Commonwealth requires the prompt amendment to the Constitution to aid those already inflicted by the Great Storms of 1976 or 1977 and any future emergency that may strike Commonwealth citizens. Therefore, the following amendment to the Constitution of the Commonwealth of Pennsylvania is proposed in accordance with the emergency provisions of Article XI thereof:

That section 17 of Article VIII be amended to read:
***

1978, MAY 16, 1977 P.L.365, J.R.4
SECTION 2. VACANCY IN EXISTING OFFICE OF ATTORNEY GENERAL.

Upon approval of this amendment by the electors, there shall be a vacancy in the office of Attorney General which shall be filled as provided herein. [151]

ENDNOTES

2. Schedule No. 1 (Adopted with the
    Constitution),
    Schedule No. 2 (Amendments of November 2,
    1909)
    Constitution of 1874.
    The Constitution of 1874 was adopted
    November 3, 1873, by a Constitutional
    Convention which was called pursuant to
    the act of April 11, 1872 (P.L.53, No.42).
    The Constitution was ratified at a special
    election held December 16, 1873, and went
    into effect January 1, 1874. This
    Constitution was amended in 1901, 1909,
    1911, 1913, 1915, 1918, 1920, 1922, 1923,
    1928, 1933, 1937, 1943, 1945, 1949, 1951,
    1953, 1955, 1956, 1957, 1958, 1959, 1961,
    1963 and 1965. By statute, 1 Pa.C.S.
    Section 906, the Constitution, as adopted
    by referendum of December 16, 1873, shall
    be known and may be cited as the
    Constitution of 1874.
    Constitution of 1968.
    The Constitution of 1874 was modified and
    renumbered by extensive amendments on
    May 17, 1966, November 8, 1966, and May
    16, 1967; and by proclamation of the
    Governor of July 7, 1967, P.L.1063,
    pursuant to the act of August 17, 1965
    (P.L.345, No.180). Proposals 1 through 7 to
    amend the Constitution were
    recommended by a Constitutional
    Convention which was called pursuant to
    the act of March 15, 1967 (P.L.2, No.2). The
    proposals were approved by the electorate
    on April 23, 1968. By statute, 1 Pa.C.S.
    Section 906, the Constitution, as amended

by referenda of May 17, 1966, November 8, 1966, May 16, 1967, and April 23, 1968, and as numbered by proclamation of the Governor of July 7, 1967, shall be known and may be cited as the Constitution of 1968.

Section Headings.

Section headings were not contained in the Constitution as adopted by referendum of December 16, 1873, but were either added by various constitutional amendments or promulgated on June 11, 1974, P.L.1573, by the Director of the Legislative Reference Bureau with the approval of the Attorney General under statutory authority contained in 1 Pa.C.S. Section 905.

Explanation of Amendment Notes.

Unless otherwise noted, amendments are referred to by date of adoption by the electorate together with a reference to the applicable joint resolution (J.R.) or, in rare cases, concurrent resolution (C.R.) adopted by the General Assembly and the page in the Laws of Pennsylvania (P.L.) in which the joint resolution or concurrent resolution was published.

2. *Adoption.* Unless otherwise noted, the provisions of Article I were adopted December 16, 1873, 1874 P.L.3, effective January 1, 1874.

3. (May 18, 1971, P.L.765, J.R.1; Nov. 3, 1998, P.L.1328, J.R.2)

4. *Constitutionality.*

The provisions of section 7 relating to criminal libel were declared unconstitutional by the Supreme Court of Pennsylvania in

Commonwealth v. Armao, 446 Pa. 325, 286 A.2d 626 (1972).

5. (Nov. 6, 1984, P.L.1306, J.R.2; Nov. 7, 1995, 1st Sp.Sess., P.L.1151, J.R.1; Nov. 4, 2003, P.L.459, J.R.1) 1995 Amendment. Joint Resolution No. 1 amended section 9. The passage of Joint Resolution No.1 was declared unconstitutional by Bergdoll v. Kane 731 A.2d 1261 (1999) and the language was reverted.

6. (Nov. 6, 1973, P.L.452, J.R.2)

7. (Nov. 3, 1998, P.L.1327, J.R.1)

8. (May 16, 1967, P.L.1035, J.R.1)

9. (May 16, 1967, P.L.1035, J.R.1)

10. (May 16, 1967, P.L.1035, J.R.1) 1967 Amendment. Joint Resolution No.1 repea ed former section 25 and renumbered former section 26 to present section 25.

11. (May 16, 1967, P.L.1035, J.R.1) 1967 Amendment. Joint Resolution No.1 added present section 26 and renumbered former section 26 to present section 25.

12. (May 18, 1971, P.L.769, J.R.3) 1971 Amendment. Joint Resolution No.3 added section 27.

13. (May 18, 1971, P.L.767, J.R.2) 1971 Amendment. Joint Resolution No.2 added section 28.

14. *Adoption.* Unless otherwise noted, the provisions of Article II were adopted December 16, 1873, 1874 P.L.3, effective January 1, 1874.

15. (Nov. 3, 1959, P.L.2158, J.R.1; May 16, 1967, P.L.1036, J.R.2)

16. (May 16, 1967, P.L.1036, J.R.2)

17. (Apr. 23, 1968, P.L.App.3, Prop. No.1)1968 Amendment. Proposal No.1 amended and consolidated former sections 16 and 17 into present section 16. The schedule to Proposal No.1 provided that section 16, if approved by

the electorate voting on April 23, 1968, shall become effective the year following that in which the next Federal decennial census is officially reported as required by Federal law.

18. (Apr. 23, 1968, P.L.App.3, Prop. No.2; Nov. 3, 1981, P.L.601, J.R.1; May 15, 2001, 2000 P.L.1057, J.R.1) 2001 Amendment. Joint Resolution No.1 of 2000 relettered subsec. (f) to subsec. (g), subsec. (g) to subsec. (h) and subsec. (h) to subsec. (i) and added a new subsec. (f). 1981 Amendment. Joint Resolution No.1 amended subsecs. (a) and (b). 1968 Amendment. Proposal No.2 amended and renumbered former section 18 to present section 17. The schedule to Proposal No.2 provided that section 17, if approved by the electorate voting on April 23, 1968, shall become effective the year following that in which the next Federal decennial census is officially reported as required by Federal law. *Prior Provisions.* Former section 17 was amended and consolidated with present section 16 by amendment of April 23, 1968, P.L.App.3, Prop. No.1.

19. *Adoption.* Unless otherwise noted, the provisions of Article III were adopted December 16, 1873, 1874 P.L.3, effective January 1, 1874. *Subdivision Headings.*
The subdivision headings of Article III were added by amendment of May 16, 1967, P.L.1037, J.R.3.

20. (May 16, 1967, P.L.1037, J.R.3)

21. (May 16, 1967, P.L.1037, J.R.3)

22. (May 16, 1967, P.L.1037, J.R.3)

23. *Prior Provisions.* Former section 7 was renumbered to present section 32 and present section 7 was renumbered from former section

8 by amendment of May 16, 1967, P.L.1037, J.R.3.

24. *Prior Provisions.* Former section 8 was renumbered to present section 7 and present section 8 was renumbered from former section 9 by amendment of May 16, 1967, P.L.1037, J.R.3.

25. *Prior Provisions.* Former section 9 was renumbered to present section 8 and present section 9 was renumbered from former section 26 by amendment of May 16, 1967, P.L.1037, J.R.3.

26. *Prior Provisions.* Former section 10 was renumbered to present section 17 and present section 10 was renumbered from former section 14 by amendment of May 16, 1967, P.L.1037, J.R.3.

27. (May 16, 1967, P.L.1037, J.R.3)
1967 Amendment. Joint Resolution No.3 renumbered former section 11 to present section 26 and amended and renumbered former section 15 to present section 11.

28. *Prior Provisions.* Former section 12 was repealed and present section 12 was renumbered from former section 25 by amendment of May 16, 1967, P.L.1037, J.R.3.

29. Prior Provisions. Former section 13 was renumbered to present section 27 and present section 13 was renumbered from former section 33 by amendment of May 16, 1967, P.L.1037, J.R.3.

30. (May 16, 1967, P.L.1037, J.R.3)
1967 Amendment. Joint Resolution No.3 renumbered former section 14 to present section 10 and amended and renumbered section 1 of former Article X (Education) to present section 14.

31. (May 16, 1967, P.L.1037, J.R.3)

1967 Amendment. Joint Resolution No.3 renumbered former section 15 to present section 11 and renumbered section 2 of former Article X (Education) to present section 15.

32. (May 16, 1967, P.L.1037, J.R.3)
1967 Amendment. Joint Resolution No.3 renumbered former section 16 to present section 24 and amended and renumbered section 1 of former Article XI (Militia) to present section 16.

33. *Prior Provisions.* Former section 17 was renumbered to present section 30 and present section 17 was renumbered from former section 10 by amendment of May 16, 1967, P.L.1037, J.R.3.

34. (Nov. 2, 1915, P.L.1103, J.R.3)
Prior Provisions. Former section 18 was renumbered to present section 29 and present section 18 was renumbered from former section 21 by amendment of May 16, 1967, P.L.1037, J.R.3.

35. (May 16, 1967, P.L.1037, J.R.3)

36. (Nov. 6, 1923, P.L.1119, J.R.3; May 16, 1967, P.L.1037, J.R.3)
1967 Amendment. Joint Resolution No.3 renumbered former section 20 to present section 31 and amended and renumbered former section 34 to present section 20. *1923 Amendment.* Joint Resolution No.3 added present section 20 (formerly section 34).

37. (Nov. 2, 1915, P.L.1104, J.R.4; May 16, 1967, P.L.1037, J.R.3)
1967 Amendment. Joint Resolution No.3 renumbered former section 21 to present section 18 and amended and numbered present section 21. *1915 Amendment.* Joint Resolution No.4 added the provisions of this section without article or section number.

38. (May 16, 1967, P.L.1037, J.R.3)
    1967 Amendment. Joint Resolution No.3 repealed former section 22 and added present section 22. The subject matter of present section 22 was formerly contained in section 12.
39. (Nov. 7, 1961, P.L.1783, J.R.1)
    Prior Provisions. Former section 24 was repealed and present section 24 was renumbered from former section 16 by amendment of May 16, 1967, P.L.1037, J R.3.
40. (Nov. 5, 1963, P.L.1401, J.R.3; May 16, 1967, P.L.1037, J.R.3)
    1967 Amendment. Joint Resolution No.3 renumbered former section 25 to present section 12 and amended and renumbered former section 35 to present section 25.
    1963 Amendment. Joint Resolution No.3 added present section 25 (formerly section 35).
41. (Nov. 8, 1955, P.L.2055, J.R.1)
    Rejection of Proposed 1981 Amendment. The question of amending section 26 to permit the General Assembly to authorize the increase of retirement benefits or pensions payable to beneficiaries who are spouses of members of a retirement or pension system, as more fully set forth in Joint Resolution No.2 of 1981, was submitted to the electors at the municipal election on November 3, 1981, and was rejected. Section 1 of Article XI prohibits the submission of an amendment more often than once in five years.
    Prior Provisions. Former section 26 was renumbered to present section 9 and present section 26 was renumbered from former section 11 by amendment of May 16, 1967, P.L.1037, J.R.3.

42. *Prior Provisions.* Former section 27 was repealed and present section 27 was renumbered from former section 13 by amendment of May 16, 1967, P.L.1037, J.R.3.
43. (May 16, 1967, P.L.1037, J.R.3)
44. (Nov. 7, 1933, P.L.1557, J.R.1; Nov. 2, 1937, P.L.2875, J.R.3-A; Nov. 5, 1963, P.L.1401, J.R.2)
    Prior Provisions. Former section 29 was repealed and present section 29 was renumbered from former section 18 by amendment of May 16, 1967, P.L.1037, J.R.3.
    Cross References. Section 29 is referred to in section 17 of Article VIII (Taxation and Finance).
45. *Prior Provisions.* Former section 30 was repealed and present section 30 was renumbered from former section 17 by amendment of May 16, 1967, P.L.1037, J.R.3.
46. (May 16, 1967, P.L.1037, J.R.3; Nov. 7, 1967, P.L.1056, J.R.9)
    1967 Amendment. Joint Resolution No.3 repealed former section 31 and renumbered former section 20 to present section 31.
47. (May 16, 1967, P.L.1037, J.R.3)
    1967 Amendment. Joint Resolution No.3 repealed former section 32 and amended and renumbered former section 7 to present section 32.
    Cross References. Section 32 is referred to in section 13 of Article IX (Local Government).
48. *Adoption.*
    Unless otherwise noted, the provisions of Article IV were adopted December 16, 1873, 1874 P.L.3, effective January 1, 1874.
49. (May 16, 1967, P.L.1044, J.R.4)
    References in Text. The Superintendent of Public Instruction, referred to in Section 1, is now the Secretary of Education

50. (May 16, 1967, P.L.1044, J.R.4)
51. (May 16, 1967, P.L.1044, J.R.4)
52. (May 16, 1978, 1977 P.L.365, J.R.4)
   1978 Amendment. Joint Resolution No.4
   added section 4.1.
   Vacancy in Existing Office.
   Section 2 of Joint Resolution No.4 provided
   that upon approval of this amendment by the
   electors, there shall be a vacancy in the office
   of Attorney General which shall be filled as
   provided herein.
53. (May 16, 1967, P.L.1044, J.R.4; May 16, 1978,
   1977 P.L.365, J.R.4)
54. (May 16, 1967, P.L.1044, J.R.4; May 16, 1978,
   1977 P.L.365, J.R.4)
55. (May 16, 1967, P.L.1044, J.R.4)
56. (Nov. 2, 1909, P.L.948, J.R.1; May 16, 1967,
   P.L.1044, J.R.4; May 20, 1975, P.L.619, J.R.1;
   May 16, 1978, 1977 P.L.365, J.R.4)
57. (May 16, 1967, P.L.1044, J.R.4; May 20, 1975,
   P.L.619, J.R.1; Nov. 4, 1997, P.L.634, J.R.2)
58. (May 16, 1967, P.L.1044, J.R.4)
59. (May 16, 1967, P.L.1044, J.R.4)
   Cross References. Section 13 is referred to in
   section 14 of this article.
60. (May 16, 1967, P.L.1044, J.R.4)
61. (May 16, 1978, 1977 P.L.365, J.R.4)
62. (May 16, 1967, P.L.1044, J.R.4)
   1967 Amendment. Joint Resolution No.4
   repealed former section 18 and added present
   section 18. The subject matter of present
   section 18 was contained in former section 21.
   Initial Terms of Office. For terms of office of
   State Treasurer and Auditor General first
   elected under present section 18, see the
   schedule to Joint Resolution No.4 of 1967 in
   the appendix to the Constitution.
63. (May 16, 1967, P.L.1044, J.R.4)

1967 Amendment. Joint Resolution No.4 repealed former section 19 and renumbered former section 22 to present section 19.

64. *Adoption.* Unless otherwise noted, the provisions of present Article V were adopted April 23, 1968, P.L.App.16, Prop. No.7, effective January 1, 1969.
Prior Provisions. Former Article V (The Judiciary) was repealed by amendment of April 23, 1968, P.L.App.16, Prop. No.7.

65. (Apr. 26, 2016, 2015 P.L.607, J.R.2)

66. (Nov. 6, 1979, P.L.581, J.R.1)
Selection of President Judge. Section 11(b) of the schedule to this article contains special provisions relating to the selection of the president judge of the Superior Court.

67. (Apr. 26, 2016, 2015 P.L.607, J.R.2)
2016 Amendment. Joint Resolution No.2 of 2015 amended the section heading and subsection (c).

68. *Cross References.* Section 9 is referred to in section 26 of the schedule to this article.

69. (Nov. 4, 2003, P.L.459, J.R.1; Apr. 26, 2016, 2015 P.L.607, J.R.2)
2016 Amendment. Joint Resolution No.2 of 2015 amended subsection (d).
2003 Amendment. Joint Resolution No.1 amended subsection (c).
Cross References. Section 10 is referred to in Sections 11, 16 of the schedule to this article.

70. *Cross Reference.* Section 11 is referred to in Section 27 of the schedule two this article.

71. (Apr. 26, 2016, 2015 P.L.607, J.R.2)
2016 Amendment. Joint Resolution No.2 of 2015 amended subsec. (b)

72. (May 20, 1975, P.L.619, J.R.1; May 16, 1978, 1977 P.L.364, J.R.3; Nov. 6, 1979, P.L.581, J.R.1)

1979 Amendment. Joint Resolution No.1 amended subsec. (b).

Appointment of Judges of Statewide Courts. The question of appointing justices and judges of statewide courts under subsec. (d) was submitted to the electors at the primary election on May 20, 1969, and was rejected. Accordingly, the Judicial Qualifications Commission does not exist.

Cross References. Section 13 is referred to in sections 14, 15 of this article; section 28 of the schedule to this article.

73. *Status of Commission.* The question of appointing justices and judges of statewide courts under section 13(d) of this article was submitted to the electors at the primary election on May 20, 1969, and was rejected. Accordingly, the Judicial Qualifications Commission does not exist.

Cross References. Section 14 is referred to in section 23 of the schedule to this article.

74. (Apr. 26, 2016, 2015 P.L.607, J.R.2) 2016 Amendment. Joint Resolution No.2 of 2015 amended subsec. (a).

Cross References. Section 15 is referred to in section 13 of this article.

75. (May 18, 1993, P.L.577, J.R.1; May 15, 2001, 2000 P.L.1057, J.R.1; Nov. 8, 2016, 2015 P.L.605, J.R.1)

2016 Amendment. Joint Resolution No.1 of 2015 amended subsec. (b).

76. Cross References. Section 17 is referred to in section 18 of this article.

77. (May 18, 1993, P.L.577, J.R.1)

1993 Amendment. Joint Resolution No.1 deleted former section 18 and added present section 18.

Cross References. Section 18 is referred to in section 16 of this article.

78. Adoption. The provisions of the Schedule to the Judiciary Article were adopted April 23, 1968, P.L.App.16, Prop. No.7, effective January 1, 1969.

This schedule is a part of this judiciary article, and it is intended that the provisions contained herein shall have the same force and effect as those contained in the numbered sections of the article. This article and schedule, unless otherwise stated herein, shall become effective on January 1, 1969. In this schedule where the word "now" appears it speaks from the date of adoption of this schedule; where the word "present" appears it speaks from the effective date hereof.

79. Partial Suspension by Statute. Section 1 (except insofar as it relates to the powers of the Supreme Court) was superseded and suspended by section 509(c) of the act of July 31, 1970 (P.L.673, No.223), known as the Appellate Court Jurisdiction Act of 1970, now repealed, and by section 26(a) of the act of July 9, 1976 (P.L.586, No.142), known as the Judiciary Act of 1976.

80. Partial Suspension by Statute. The first sentence of section 2 was superseded and suspended by section 509(c) of the act of July 31, 1970 (P.L.673, No.223), known as the Appellate Court Jurisdiction Act of 1970, now repealed, and by section 26(a) of the act of July 9, 1976 (P.L.586, No.142), known as the Judiciary Act of 1976.

81. Suspension by Statute. Section 4 was superseded and suspended in part by section 509(c) of the act of July 31, 1970 (P.L.673, No.223), known as the Appellate Court

167

Jurisdiction Act of 1970, now repealed, and was superseded and suspended by section 26(a) of the act of July 9, 1976 (P.L.586, No.142), known as the Judiciary Act of 1976.

82. (Nov. 6, 1979, P.L.581, J.R.1)

83. *Suspension by Statute.* Section 13 was superseded and suspended by Section 26(a) of the act of July 9, 1976 (P.L.586, No.142), known as the Judiciary Act of 1976.

    References in Text. The Department of Public Instruction, referred to in Section 13(d), is now the Department of Education.

84. Partial Suspension by Statute. Subsections (a), (b),

    (c), (d), (e), (f), (g), (h), (i), (j), (r), (s), (t), (u), (w) and (except as provided in section 22 of Act 142 of 1976) (z) of section 16 were superseded and suspended by section 26(a) of the act of July 9, 1976 (P.L.586, No.142), known as the Judiciary Act of 1976, and, effective upon the date upon which the provision is or was suspended by general rule, subsections (o), (p) and (q) of section 16 were superseded and suspended by section 26(b) of Act 142.

85. Suspension by Statute. Section 17 was superseded and suspended by section 26(b) of the act of July 9, 1976 (P.L.586, No.142), known as the Judiciary Act of 1976, effective upon the date upon which the provision is or was suspended by general rule.

86. Suspension by Statute. Section 18 was superseded and suspended by section 26(a) of the act of July 9, 1976 (P.L.586, No.142), known as the Judiciary Act of 1976.

87. Suspension by Statute. Section 20 was superseded and suspended by section 26(a) of the act of July 9, 1976 (P.L.586, No.142),

known as the Judiciary Act of 1976.

Cross References. Section 20 is referred to in Section 19 of this schedule.

88. Suspension by Statute. Section 21 was superseded and suspended by section 26(a) of the act of July 9, 1976 (P.L.586, No.142), known as the Judiciary Act of 1976.

89. *Status of Commission.* The question of appointing justices and judges of statewide courts under section 13(d) of this article was submitted to the electors at the primary election on May 20, 1969, and was rejected. Accordingly, the Judicial Qualifications Commission does not exist.

90. (May 18, 1993, P.L.577, J.R.1)

91. *Suspension by Statute.* Section 25 was superseded and suspended by section 26(b) of the act of July 9, 1976 (P.L.586, No.142), known as the Judiciary Act of 1976, effective upon the date upon which the provision is or was suspended by general rule.*Partial Suspension by Court Rule.* Section 25 was suspended November 5, 1975, by Pennsylvania Rule of Appellate Procedure No. 5105(g), effective July 1, 1976, insofar as inconsistent with the Rules of Appellate Procedure. By amendment of December 11, 1978, effective December 30, 1978, the former provisions of Rule No. 5105(g) are now contained in Rule No. 5101(d).

92. *Suspension by Statute.* Section 27 was superseded and suspended by section 26(a) of the act of July 9, 1976 (P.L.586, No.142), known as the Judiciary Act of 1976.

93. *Status of Commission.* The question of appointing justices and judges of statewide courts under section 13(d) of this article was

submitted to the electors at the primary election on May 20, 1969, and was rejected. Accordingly, the Judicial Qualifications Commission does not exist.

94. *Adoption.* Unless otherwise noted, the provisions of present Article VI (formerly Article XII) were adopted December 16, 1873, 1874 P.L.3, effective January 1, 1874, and the article was renumbered from XII to VI by proclamation of the Governor of July 7, 1967, P.L.1063. See also proclamation of the Governor of July 14, 1966, 1965 P.L.1945.

Prior Provisions. Former Article VI was repealed by amendment of May 17, 1966, 1965 P.L.1928, J.R.10. The subject matter of present Article VI was formerly contained in Articles VI (Impeachment and Removal from Office), VII (Oath of Office) and XII (Public Officers).

Cross References. Article VI is referred to in sections 16, 18 of Article V (The Judiciary).

95. (Nov. 2, 1909, P.L.948, J.R.1; May 17, 1966, 1965 P.L.1928, J.R.10)

1966 Amendment. Joint Resolution No.10 renumbered former section 1 of this article to present Section 4 and amended and renumbered section 1 of former Article XII to present Section 1.

96. (May 17, 1966, 1965 P.L.1928, J.R.10)

1966 Amendment. Joint Resolution No.10 renumbered former Section 2 of this article to present section 5 and renumbered section 2 of former Article XII to present Section 2.

97. (May 17, 1966, 1965 P.L.1928, J.R.10)

1966 Amendment. Joint Resolution No.10 renumbered former section 3 to present section 6 and added present Section 3.

98. (May 17, 1966, 1965 P.L.1928, J.R.10)

1966 Amendment. Joint Resolution No.10 renumbered former section 4 to present section 7 and renumbered former section 1 to present
section 4.

99. (May 17, 1966, 1965 P.L.1928, J.R.10)
1966 Amendment. Joint Resolution No.10 amended and renumbered former section 2 to present
section 5.

100. (May 17, 1966, 1965 P.L.1928, J.R.10)
1966 Amendment. Joint Resolution No.10 amended and renumbered former section 3 to present section 6.

101. (May 17, 1966, 1965 P.L.1928, J.R.10)
Constitutionality. A statute that conflicts with the removal provisions provided under this section is unconstitutional unless the statute that provides for the alternative removal process predates this section. See South Newton Township Electors v. Bouch , 838 A.2d 643 (Pa. 2003).
1966 Amendment. Joint Resolution No.10 amended and renumbered former section 4 to present
section 7.

102. *Adoption.* Unless otherwise noted, the provisions of
present Article VII (formerly Article VIII) were adopted December 16, 1873, 1874 P.L.3, effective January 1, 1874. The present article heading was amended May 16, 1967, P.L.1048, J.R.5, and the article was renumbered from VIII to VII by proclamation of the Governor of July 7, 1967, P.L.1063.
Prior Provisions. Former Article VII (Oath of Office) was repealed by amendment of May 17, 1966, 1965 P.L.1928, J.R.10. The subject

matter is now contained in section 3 of Article VI (Public Officers).

103. (Nov. 5, 1901, P.L.881, J.R.1; Nov. 7, 1933, P.L.1559, J.R.5; Nov. 3, 1959, P.L.2160, J.R.3; May 16, 1967, P.L.1048, J.R.5)

Age of Electors. The age at which a citizen is entitled to vote was changed from 21 to 18 years of age. See Amendment XXVI to the Constitution of the United States and section 701 of the act of June 3, 1937 (P.L.1333, No.320), known as the Pennsylvania Election Code.

104. (Nov. 2, 1909, P.L.948, J.R.1; May 16, 1967, P.L.1048, J.R.5)

105. (Nov. 2, 1909, P.L.948, J.R.1; Nov. 4, 1913, P.L.1477, C.R.3; May 16, 1967, P.L.1048, J.R.5)

106. (Nov. 5, 1901, P.L.882, J.R.2)

107. (Nov. 5, 1901, P.L.881, J.R.1; Nov. 6, 1928, 1927 P.L.1050, J.R.13; May 16, 1967, P.L.1048, J.R.5)

1967 Amendment. Joint Resolution No.5 repealed former section 6 and amended and renumbered former section 7 to present section 6.

108. *Prior Provisions.* Former section 7 was renumbered to present section 6 and present section 7 was renumbered from former section 8 by amendment of May 16, 1967, P.L.1048, J.R.5.

109. Prior Provisions. Former section 8 was renumbered to present section 7 and present section 8 was renumbered from former section 10 by amendment of May 16, 1967, P.L.1048, J.R.5.

110. (Nov. 6, 1928, 1927 P.L.1043, J.R.6; Nov. 2, 1943, P.L.917, J.R.1)

Prior Provisions. Former section 9 was repealed and present section 9 was renumbered from former section 11 by amendment of May 16, 1967, P.L.1048, J.R.5.

111. (May 16, 1967, P.L.1048, J.R.5)
1967 Amendment. Joint Resolution No.5 renumbered former section 10 to present section 8 and amended and renumbered former section 12 to present section 10.

112. (Nov. 6, 1945, P.L.1419, J.R.3; May 16, 1967, P.L.1048, J.R.5)
1967 Amendment. Joint Resolution No.5 renumbered former section 11 to present section 9 and renumbered former section 14 to present section 11.

113. (May 16, 1967, P.L.1048, J.R.5)
1967 Amendment. Joint Resolution No.5 renumbered former section 12 to present section 10 and amended and renumbered former section 15 to present section 12.

114. (May 16, 1967, P.L.1048, J.R.5)
1967 Amendment. Joint Resolution No.5 repealed former section 13 and amended and renumbered former section 17 to present section 13.

115. (Nov. 5, 1957, P.L.1019, J.R.1; May 16, 1967, P.L.1048, J.R.5; Nov. 5, 1985, P.L.555, J.R.1; Nov. 4, 1997, P.L.636, J.R.3)
1967 Amendment. Joint Resolution No.5 renumbered former section 14 to present section 11 and amended and renumbered former section 19 to present section 14.
1957 Amendment. Joint Resolution No.1 added present section 14 (formerly section 19).

116. Adoption. Unless otherwise noted, the provisions of present Article VIII (formerly Article IX) were adopted December 16, 1873,

173

1874 P.L.3, effective January 1, 1874. The article number was changed from IX to VIII by proclamation of the Governor of July 7, 1967, P.L.1063.

Prior Provisions. Former Article VIII (Suffrage and Elections) was renumbered to Article VII by proclamation of the Governor of July 7, 1967, P.L.1063.

117. (Nov. 6, 1923, P.L.1117, J.R.1; Nov. 4, 1958, 1957 P.L.1021, J.R.3; Nov. 7, 1961, P.L.1785, J.R.6; Nov. 2, 1965, P.L.1908, J.R.2; Apr. 23, 1968, P.L.App.9, Prop. No.5)

1968 Amendment. Section 4 of Proposal No.5 provided that the amendment to section 1 shall take effect as soon as possible but no later than July 1, 1970.

118. (Apr. 23, 1968, P.L.App.9, Prop. No.5; May 15, 1973, P.L.451, J.R.1; Nov. 8, 1977, P.L.361, J.R.1; Nov. 6, 1984, 1982 P.L.1478, J.R.2; Nov. 5, 1985, P.L.556, J.R.2; Nov. 4, 1997, P.L.633, J.R.1; Nov. 7, 2017, 2018 P.L.1197, J.R.1)

2018 Amendment. Joint Resolution No.1 of 2017 amended subsec. (b)(vi).

Rejection of Proposed 1989 Amendment. The question of amending subsection (b) to permit local taxing authorities to reduce tax rates on residential real property to the extent of additional revenues obtained from personal income taxes, as more fully set forth in Joint Resolution No.1 of 1989, was submitted to the electors at the municipal election on May 16, 1989, and was rejected. Section 1 of Article XI prohibits the submission of an amendment more often than once in five years.

1985 Amendment. Joint Resolution No.2 amended subsec. (c).

1984 Amendment. Joint Resolution No.2 of 1982 added subsec. (b)(v).

1973 Amendment. Joint Resolution No.1 amended subsec. (b)(i).

1968 Amendment. Proposal No.5 renumbered former section 2 to present section 5 and added present section 2. Section 4 of Proposal No.5 provided that section 2 shall take effect as soon as possible but no later than July 1, 1970.

119. (Nov. 6, 1928, 1927 P.L.1049, J.R.12)

1928 Amendment. Joint Resolution No.12 added present section 3 (formerly section 1B). Prior Provisions. Former section 3 was renumbered to present section 6 and present section 3 was renumbered from section 1B by amendment of April 23, 1968, P.L.App.9, Prop. No.5.

120. (Apr. 23, 1968, P.L.App.9, Prop. No.5)

1968 Amendment. Proposal No.5 added present section 4. Section 4 of Proposal No.5 provided that section 4 shall take effect July 1, 1970, unless the General Assembly earlier provides enabling legislation in accordance therewith.

Prior Provisions. Former section 4 was both repealed and renumbered to present section 7 by amendment of April 23, 1968, P.L.App.5, Prop. No.3.

121. Prior Provisions. Former section 5 was repealed by amendment of April 23, 1968, P.L.App.5, Prop. No.3, and present section 5 was renumbered from former section 2 by amendment of April 23, 1968, P.L.App.9, Prop. No.5.

122. (Apr. 23, 1968, P.L.App.9, Prop. No.5)

1968 Amendment. Proposal No.5 amended and renumbered former section 3 to present section 6.

Prior Provisions. Former section 6 was renumbered to present section 8 by amendment of April 23, 1968, P.L.App.5, Prop. No.3.

123. (Nov. 5, 1918, 1917 P.L.1264, J.R.1; Nov. 6, 1923, P.L.1118, J.R.2; Apr. 23, 1968, P.L.App.5, Prop. No.3)

1968 Amendment. Proposal No.3 amended and renumbered former section 4 to present section 7.

Prior Provisions. Former section 7 was repealed by amendment of April 23, 1968, P.L.App.11, Prop. No.6.

Cross References. Section 7 is referred to in sections 15, 16 of this article.

124. (Apr. 23, 1968, P.L.App.5, Prop. No.3)

1968 Amendment. Proposal No.3 amended and renumbered former section 6 to present section 8.

Prior Provisions. Former section 8 was repealed by amendment of April 23, 1968, P.L.App.11, Prop. No.6.

125. (Apr. 23, 1968, P.L.App.5, Prop. No.3)

126. (Apr. 23, 1968, P.L.App.7, Prop. No.4)

1968 Amendment. Proposal No.4 amended and renumbered former section 14 to present section 10. Section 3 of Proposal No.4 provided that section 10 shall take effect as soon as possible but no later than July 1, 1970.

Prior Provisions. Former section 10 was repealed by amendment of April 23, 1968, P.L.App.11, Prop. No.6.

127. (Nov. 6, 1945, P.L.1418, J.R.1; Nov. 3, 1981, P.L.603, J.R.2)

1981 Amendment. Joint Resolution No.2 amended and lettered existing provisions subsec. (a) and added subsec. (b).

1945 Amendment. Joint Resolution No.1 added present section 11 (formerly section 18).

Prior Provisions. Former section 11 was repealed by amendment of April 23, 1968, P.L.App.5, Prop. No.3, and present section 11 was renumbered from former section 18 by amendment of April 23, 1968, P.L.App.9, Prop. No.5.

128. (Apr. 23, 1968, P.L.App.7, Prop. No.4)
1968 Amendment. Proposal No.4 added present section 12. Section 3 of Proposal No.4 provided that section 12 shall take effect as soon as possible but no later than July 1, 1970.

Prior Provisions. Former section 12 was repealed by amendment of April 23, 1968, P.L.App.5,
Prop. No.3.

129. (Apr. 23, 1968, P.L.App.7, Prop. No.4)
1968 Amendment. Proposal No.4 added present section 13. Section 3 of Proposal No.4 provided that section 13 shall take effect as soon as possible but no later than July 1, 1970.

Prior Provisions. Former section 13 was repealed by amendment of April 23, 1968, P.L.App.5,
Prop. No.3.

130. (Apr. 23, 1968, P.L.App.7, Prop. No.4)
1968 Amendment. Proposal No.4 renumbered former section 14 to present section 10 and added present section 14. Section 3 of Proposal No.4 provided that section 14 shall take effect as soon as possible but no later than July 1, 1970.

131. (Nov. 5, 1963, P.L.1403, J.R.5)

1963 Amendment. Joint Resolution No.5 added present section 15 (formerly section 24).

Prior Provisions. Former section 15 was repealed by amendment of April 23, 1968, P.L.App.11, Prop. No.6, and present section 15 was renumbered from section 24 by amendment of April 23, 1968, P.L.App.9, Prop. No.5.

Repeal of Section. Section 4 of Proposal No.3 of 1968 provided that, effective when the last bonds have been issued under its authority, section 24 (now section 15) is repealed.

Cross References. Section 15 is referred to in section 16 of this article.

132. (May 16, 1967, P.L.1055, J.R.8)

1967 Amendment. Joint Resolution No.8 added present section 16 (formerly section 25).

Prior Provisions. Former section 16 was repealed by amendment of April 23, 1968, P.L.App.5, Prop. No.3, and present section 16 was renumbered from section 25 by amendment of April 23, 1968, P.L.App.9, Prop. No.5.

Repeal of Section. Section 4 of Proposal No.3 of 1968 provided that, effective when the last bonds have been issued under its authority, section 25 (now section 16) is repealed.

133. (Nov. 7, 1972, 1st Sp.Sess., P.L.1970, J.R.1; P.L.622, J.R.2; Nov. 8, 1977, P.L.362, J.R.2) apply of an emergency Nov. 4, 1975,

1977 Amendment. Joint Resolution No.2 amended and lettered existing provisions subsec. (a) and added subsec. (b) under the emergency provisions of Article XI. For preamble to amendment, see section 1 of

Joint Resolution No.2 in the appendix to the Constitution.

1975 Amendment. Joint Resolution No.2 amended section 17 under the emergency provisions of section 1(a) and (b) of Article XI. For preamble to amendment, see section 1 of Joint Resolution No.2 in the appendix to the Constitution.

1972 Amendment. Joint Resolution No.1 added present section 17 under the emergency provisions of section 1(a) and (b) of Article XI. For preamble to amendment, see section 1 of Joint Resolution No.1 in the appendix to the Constitution.

Prior Provisions. Former section 17 was repealed by amendment of April 23, 1968, P.L.App.5, Prop. No.3.

134. Adoption. Unless otherwise noted, the provisions of present Article IX were adopted April 23, 1968, P.L. App.11, Prop. No.6. For effective date of 1968 amendment, see section 3 of Proposal No.6 of 1968 in the appendix to the Constitution. Prior Provisions. Former Article IX was renumbered Article VIII by proclamation of the Governor of July 7, 1967, P.L.1063. The subject matter of present Article IX was contained in part in former Articles IX (Taxation and Finance), XIII (New Counties), XIV (County Officers) and XV (Cities and City Charters).

135. Interpretation of Section. Section 3 of Proposal No.6 of 1968 provided that the second sentence of section 1 shall be construed so as to be consistent with the jurisdiction of the Constitutional Convention.

136. Cross References. Section 2 is referred to in section 13 of this article.

137. Interpretation of Section. Section 3 of Proposal No.6 of 1968 provided that the first paragraph of Section 8 on Uniform Legislation shall be construed so as to be consistent with the jurisdiction of the Constitutional Convention.

138. Adoption. Present Article X was adopted (without article number) November 8, 1966, 1965 P.L.1909, J.R.3, and the article number was supplied by proclamation of the Governor of July 7, 1967, P.L.1063.

Prior Provisions. Former Article X (Education) was repealed and former sections 1 and 2 were transferred to sections 14 and 15, respectively, of Article III (Legislation) by amendment of May 16, 1967, P.L.1037, J.R.3. The subject matter of present Article X was formerly contained in Article XVI which was repealed by amendment of November 8, 1966, 1965 P.L.1909, J.R.3.

139. *Adoption.* Unless otherwise noted, the provisions of present Article XI (formerly Article XVIII) were adopted December 16, 1873, 1874 P.L.3, effective January 1, 1874. The present article heading was amended on May 16, 1967, P.L.1052, J.R.6, and the article was renumbered from XVIII to XI by proclamation of the Governor of July 7, 1967, P.L.1063.

Prior Provisions. Former Article XI (Militia) was repealed and its provisions (section 1) transferred to section 16 of Article III (Legislation) by amendment of May 16, 1967, P.L.1037, J.R.3.

140. (May 16, 1967, P.L.1052, J.R.6)
1967 Amendment. Joint Resolution No.6 added subsecs. (a) and (b).

141. *Adoption.* The provisions of Schedule No.1 were adopted December 16, 1873, 1874 P.L.3, effective January 1, 1874.
Partial Repeal of Schedule. See section 2 of Proposal No.7 of 1968 in the appendix to the Constitution for provisions relating to the partial repeal of Schedule No.1.
142. *Adoption.* The provisions of Schedule No.2 were adopted November 2, 1909, P.L.948, J.R.1.Partial Repeal of Schedule. See section 2 of Proposal No.7 of 1968 in the appendix to the Constitution for provisions relating to the partial repeal of Schedule No.2.
143. *Explanatory Note.* Joint Resolution No.4 added section 18 and made other changes in Article IV.
144. *Explanatory Note.* Proposal No.1 amended and consolidated former sections 16 and 17 into present section 16 of Article II.
145. *Explanatory Note.* Proposal No.2 amended and renumbered former section 18 to present section 17 of Article II.
146. *References in Text.* Sections 24 and 25 were renumbered to present sections 15 and 16, respectively, of Article VIII by Proposal No.5 of 1968.

147. *Explanatory Note.* Proposal No.5 amended section 1, added sections 2 and 4 and renumbered or amended other sections of Article VIII.
148. *Explanatory Note.* Proposal No.6 added present Article IX and repealed sections in Articles VIII, XIII, XIV and XV.
149. *Explanatory Note*. Proposal No.7 added present Article V.

150. *Explanatory Note.* Joint Resolution No.1 added section 17 of Article VIII.
151. *Explanatory Note.* Joint Resolution No.4 added section 4.1 and amended sections 5, 6, 8 and 17 of Article IV.

The United States Constitution

The Preamble
We the People of the United States, in Order to form a more perfect Union, establish Justice, insure domestic Tranquility, provide for the common defense, promote the general Welfare, and secure the Blessings of Liberty to ourselves and our Posterity, do ordain and establish this Constitution for the United States of America.Bibliography

ARTICLE I

SECTION 1
All legislative Powers herein granted shall be vested in a Congress of the United States, which shall consist of a Senate and House of Representatives.

SECTION 2
The House of Representatives shall be composed of Members chosen every second Year by the People of the several States, and the Electors in each State shall have the Qualifications requisite for Electors of the most numerous Branch of the State Legislature.

No Person shall be a Representative who shall not have attained to the Age of twenty five Years, and been seven Years a Citizen of the United States, and who shall not, when elected, be an Inhabitant of that State in which he shall be chosen.

Representatives and direct Taxes shall be apportioned among the several States which may be included within this Union, according to their respective Numbers, which shall be determined by adding to the whole Number of free Persons, including those bound to Service for a Term of Years, and excluding Indians not taxed, three fifths of all other Persons. The actual Enumeration shall be made within three Years after the first Meeting of the Congress of the United States, and within every subsequent Term of ten Years, in such Manner as they shall by Law direct. The Number of Representatives shall not exceed one for every thirty Thousand, but each State shall have at Least one Representative; and until such enumeration shall be made, the State of New Hampshire shall be entitled to choose three, Massachusetts eight, Rhode Island and Providence Plantations one, Connecticut five, New-York six, New Jersey four, Pennsylvania eight, Delaware one, Maryland six, Virginia ten, North Carolina five, South Carolina five, and Georgia three.

When vacancies happen in the Representation from any State, the Executive Authority thereof shall issue Writs of Election to fill such Vacancies.

The House of Representatives shall choose their Speaker and other Officers; and shall have the sole Power of Impeachment.

SECTION 3
The Senate of the United States shall be composed of two Senators from each State, chosen by the Legislature thereof, for six Years; and each Senator shall have one Vote.

Immediately after they shall be assembled in Consequence of the first Election, they shall be divided as equally as may be into three classes. The

Seats of the Senators of the first Class shall be vacated at the Expiration of the second Year, of the second Class at the Expiration of the fourth Year, and of the third Class at the Expiration of the sixth Year, so that one third may be chosen every second Year; and if Vacancies happen by Resignation or otherwise, during the Recess of the Legislature of any State, the Executive thereof may make temporary Appointments until the next Meeting of the Legislature, which shall then fill such Vacancies.

No Person shall be a Senator who shall not have attained to the Age of thirty Years, and been nine Years a Citizen of the United States, and who shall not, when elected, be an Inhabitant of that State for which he shall be chosen.

The Vice President of the United States shall be President of the Senate, but shall have no Vote, unless they be equally divided.

The Senate shall choose their other Officers, and also a President *pro tempore*, in the Absence of the Vice President, or when he shall exercise the Office of President of the United States.
The Senate shall have the sole Power to try all Impeachments. When sitting for that Purpose, they shall be on Oath or Affirmation. When the President of the United States is tried, the Chief Justice shall preside: And no Person shall be convicted without the Concurrence of two thirds of the Members present.

Judgment in Cases of Impeachment shall not extend further than to removal from Office, and disqualification to hold and enjoy any Office of honor, Trust or Profit under the United States: but the Party convicted shall nevertheless be liable and subject to Indictment, Trial, Judgment and Punishment, according to Law.

SECTION 4
The Times, Places and Manner of holding Elections for Senators and Representatives, shall be prescribed in each State by the Legislature thereof; but the Congress may at any time by Law make or alter such Regulations, except as to the Places of choosing Senators.

The Congress shall assemble at least once in every Year, and such Meeting shall be on the first Monday in December, unless they shall by Law appoint a different Day.

SECTION 5
Each House shall be the Judge of the Elections, Returns and Qualifications of its own Members, and a Majority of each shall constitute a Quorum to do Business; but a smaller Number may adjourn from day to day, and may be authorized to compel the Attendance of absent Members, in such Manner, and under such Penalties as each House may provide.

Each House may determine the Rules of its Proceedings, punish its Members for disorderly Behavior, and, with the Concurrence of two thirds, expel a Member.

Each House shall keep a Journal of its Proceedings and from time to time publish the same, excepting such Parts as may in their Judgment require Secrecy; and the Yeas and Nays of the Members of either House on any question shall, at the Desire of one fifth of those Present, be entered on the Journal.

Neither House, during the Session of Congress, shall, without the Consent of the other, adjourn for more than three days, nor to any other Place than that in which the two Houses shall be sitting.

SECTION 6

The Senators and Representatives shall receive a Compensation for their Services, to be ascertained by Law, and paid out of the Treasury of the United States. They shall in all Cases, except Treason, Felony and Breach of the Peace, be privileged from Arrest during their Attendance at the Session of their respective Houses and in going to and returning from the same; and for any Speech or Debate in either House, they shall not be questioned n any other Place.

No Senator or Representative shall, during the Time for which he was elected, be appointed to any civil Office under the Authority of the United States, which shall have been created, or the Emoluments whereof shall have been increased during such time; and no Person holding any Office under the United States, shall be a Member of either House during his Continuance in Office.

SECTION 7

All Bills for raising Revenue shall originate in the House of Representatives; but the Senate may propose or concur with Amendments as or other Bills.

Every Bill which shall have passed the House of Representatives and the Senate, shall, before it become a Law, be presented to the President of the United States; If he approve he shall sign it, but if not he shall return it, with his Objections to that House in which it shall have originated, who shall enter the Objections at large on their Journal, and proceed to reconsider it. If after such Reconsideration two thirds of that House shall agree to pass the Bill, it shall be sent, together with the Objections, to the other House, by which it shall likewise be reconsidered, and if approved by two thirds of that House, it shall become a Law. But in all such Cases the Votes of both Houses shall be determined by yeas and Nays, and the Names of the Persons voting for and against the Bill shall be entered on the Journal of each House respectively. If any Bill shall not be returned by the President within ten Days (Sundays excepted) after it shall have been presented to him, the Same shall be a Law, in like Manner as if he had signed it, unless the Congress by their Adjournment prevent its Return, in which Case it shall not be a Law.

Every Order, Resolution, or Vote to which the Concurrence of the Senate and House of Representatives may be necessary (except on a question of Adjournment) shall be presented to the President of the United States; and before the Same shall take Effect, shall be approved by him, or being disapproved by him, shall be repassed by two thirds of the Senate and House of Representatives, according to the Rules and Limitation prescribed in the Case of a Bill.

SECTION 8
The Congress shall have Power To lay and collect Taxes, Duties, Imposts and Excises, to pay the Debts and provide for the common Defense and general Welfare of the United States; but all Duties, Imposts and Excises shall be uniform throughout the United States;

To borrow Money on the credit of the United States;

To regulate Commerce with foreign Nations and among the several States, and with the Indian Tribes;

To establish an uniform Rule of Naturalization, and uniform Laws on the subject of Bankruptcies throughout the United States;

To coin Money, regulate the Value thereof, and of foreign Coin, and fix the Standard of Weights and Measures;

To provide for the Punishment of counterfeiting the Securities and current Coin of the United States;

To establish Post Offices and post Roads;

To promote the Progress of Science and useful Arts, by securing for limited Times to Authors and Inventors the exclusive Right to their respective Writings and Discoveries;

To constitute Tribunals inferior to the supreme Court;

To define and punish Piracies and Felonies committed on the high Seas, and Offenses against the Law of Nations;

To declare War, grant Letters of Marque and Reprisal, and make Rules concerning Captures on Land and Water;

To raise and support Armies, but no Appropriation of Money to that Use shall be for a longer Term than two Years;

To provide and maintain a Navy;

To make Rules for the Government and Regulation of the land and naval Forces;

To provide for calling forth the Militia to execute the Laws of the Union, suppress Insurrections and repel Invasions;

To provide for organizing, arming, and disciplining, the Militia, and for governing such Part of them as may be employed in the Service of the United States, reserving to the States respectively, the Appointment of the Officers, and the Authority of training the Militia according to the discipline prescribed by Congress;

To exercise exclusive Legislation in all Cases whatsoever, over such District (not exceeding ten Miles square) as may, by Cession of particular States, and the Acceptance of Congress, become the Seat of Government of the United States, and to exercise like Authority over all Places purchased by the Consent of the Legislature of the State in which the Same shall be, for the Erection of Forts, Magazines, Arsenals, dock-Yards, and other needful Buildings;–And

To make all Laws which shall be necessary and proper for carrying into Execution the foregoing Powers, and all other Powers vested by this Constitution in the Government of the United States, or in any Department or Officer thereof.

SECTION 9
The Migration or Importation of such Persons as any of the States now existing shall think proper to admit, shall not be prohibited by the Congress prior

to the Year one thousand eight hundred and eight, but a Tax or duty may be imposed on such Importation, not exceeding ten dollars for each Person.

The Privilege of the Writ of Habeas Corpus shall not be suspended, unless when in Cases of Rebellion or Invasion the public Safety may require it.

No Bill of Attainder or ex post facto Law shall be passed.

No Capitation, or other direct, Tax shall be laid, unless in Proportion to the Census or enumeration herein before directed to be taken.

No Tax or Duty shall be laid on Articles exported from any State.

No Preference shall be given by any Regulation of Commerce or Revenue to the Ports of one State over those of another: nor shall Vessels bound to, or from, one State, be obliged to enter, clear, or pay duties in another.

No Money shall be drawn from the Treasury but in Consequence of Appropriations made by Law; and a regular Statement and Account of the Receipts and Expenditures of all public Money shall be published from time to time.

No Title of Nobility shall be granted by the United States: And no Person holding any Office of Profit or Trust under them, shall, without the Consent of the Congress accept of any present, Emolument, Office, or Title, of any kind whatever, from any King, Prince, or foreign State.

SECTION 10

No State shall enter into any Treaty, Alliance, or Confederation; grant Letters of Marque and Reprisal; coin Money; emit Bills of Credit; make any Thing but gold and silver Coin a Tender in Payment of Debts; pass any Bill of Attainder, ex post facto Law, or Law impairing the Obligation of Contracts, or grant any Title of Nobility.

No State shall, without the Consent of the Congress, lay any Imposts or Duties on Imports or Exports, except what may be absolutely necessary for executing it's inspection Laws: and the net Produce of all Duties and Imposts, laid by any State on Imports or Exports, shall be for the Use of the Treasury of the United States; and all such Laws shall be subject to the Revision and Control of the Congress.

No State shall, without the Consent of Congress, lay any Duty of Tonnage, keep Troops, or Ships of War in time of Peace, enter into any Agreement or Compact with another State, or with a foreign Power, or engage in War, unless actually invaded, or in such imminent Danger as will not admit of delay.

ARTICLE II

SECTION 1

The executive Power shall be vested in a President of the United States of America. He shall hold his Office during the Term of four Years, and, together with the Vice President, chosen for the same Term, be elected, as follows

Each State shall appoint, in such Manner as the Legislature thereof may direct, a Number of Electors, equal to the whole Number of Senators and Representatives to which the State may be entitled in the Congress: but no Senator or Representative, or Person holding an Office of Trust or Profit under the United States, shall be appointed an Elector.

The Electors shall meet in their respective States, and vote by Ballot for two Persons, of whom one at least shall not be an Inhabitant of the same State with themselves. And they shall make a List of all the Persons voted for, and of the Number of Votes for each; which List they shall sign and certify, and transmit sealed to the Seat of the Government of the United States, directed to the President of the Senate. The President of the Senate shall, in the presence of the Senate and House of Representatives, open all the Certificates, and the Votes shall then be counted. The Person having the greatest Number of Votes shall be the President, if such Number be a Majority of the whole Number of Electors appointed; and if there be more than one who have such Majority, and have an equal Number of Votes, then the House of Representatives shall immediately choose by Ballot one of them for President; and if no Person have a Majority, then from the five highest on the List the said House shall in like manner choose the President. But in choosing the President, the Votes shall be taken by States, the Representation from each State having one Vote; A quorum for this Purpose shall consist of a Member or Members from two thirds of the States, and a Majority of all the States shall be necessary to a Choice. In every Case, after the Choice of the President, the Person having the greatest Number of Votes of the Electors shall be the Vice President. But if there should remain two or more who have equal

Votes, the Senate shall choose from them by Ballot the Vice President.

The Congress may determine the Time of choosing the Electors, and the Day on which they shall give their Votes; which Day shall be the same throughout the United States.

No Person except a natural born Citizen, or a Citizen of the United States, at the time of the Adoption of this Constitution, shall be eligible to the Office of President; neither shall any Person be eligible to that Office who shall not have attained to the Age of thirty five Years, and been fourteen Years a Resident within the United States.

In Case of the Removal of the President from Office, or of his Death, Resignation, or Inability to discharge the Powers and Duties of the said Office, the Same shall devolve on the Vice President, and the Congress may by law provide for the Case of Removal, Death, Resignation or Inability, both of the President and Vice President, declaring what Officer shall then act as President, and such Officer shall act accordingly, until the Disability be removed, or a President shall be elected.

The President shall, at stated Times, receive for his Services, a Compensation, which shall neither be increased nor diminished during the Period for which he shall have been elected, and he shall not receive within that Period any other Emolument from the United States, or any of them.

Before he enter on the Execution of his Office, he shall take the following Oath or Affirmation:– *I do solemnly swear (or affirm) that I will faithfully execute the Office of President of the United States, and will to the best of my Ability, preserve, protect and defend the Constitution of the United States.*

SECTION 2

The President shall be Commander in Chief of the Army and Navy of the United States, and of the Militia of the several States, when called into the actual Service of the United States; he may require the Opinion, in writing, of the principal Officer in each of the executive Departments, upon any Subject relating to the Duties of their respective Offices, and he shall have Power to grant Reprieves and Pardons for Offenses against the United States, except in Cases of Impeachment.

He shall have Power, by and with the Advice and Consent of the Senate, to make Treaties, provided two thirds of the Senators present concur; and he shall nominate, and by and with the Advice and Consent of the Senate, shall appoint Ambassadors, other public Ministers and Consuls, Judges of the supreme Court, and all other Officers of the United States, whose Appointments are not herein otherwise provided for, and which shall be established by Law: but the Congress may by Law vest the Appointment of such inferior Officers, as they think proper, in the President alone, in the Courts of Law, or in the Heads of Departments.

The President shall have Power to fill up all Vacancies that may happen during the Recess of the Senate, by granting Commissions which shall expire at the End of their next Session.

SECTION 3

He shall from time to time give to the Congress Information of the State of the Union, and recommend to their Consideration such Measures as he shall judge necessary and expedient; he may, on extraordinary Occasions, convene both Houses, or either of them, and in Case of Disagreement between them, with Respect to the Time of Adjournment, he may adjourn them to such Time as he shall think proper; he shall receive Ambassadors and other public Ministers; he shall take Care that the Laws be faithfully executed, and shall Commission all the Officers of the United States.

SECTION 4

The President, Vice President and all civil Officers of the United States, shall be removed from Office on Impeachment for, and Conviction of, Treason, Bribery, or other high Crimes and Misdemeanors.

ARTICLE III

SECTION 1

The judicial Power of the United States, shall be vested in one supreme Court, and in such inferior Courts as the Congress may from time to time ordain and establish. The Judges, both of the supreme and inferior Courts, shall hold their Offices during good Behaviour, and shall, at stated Times, receive for their Services, a Compensation, which shall not be diminished during their Continuance in Office.

SECTION 2

The Judicial Power shall extend to all Cases, in Law and Equity, arising under this Constitution, the Laws of the United States, and Treaties made, or which shall be made, under their Authority;—to all Cases affecting Ambassadors, other public Ministers and Consuls;—to all Cases of admiralty and maritime Jurisdiction;—to Controversies to which the United States shall be a Party;—to Controversies between two or more States;—between a State and Citizens of another State;—between Citizens of different States,—between Citizens of the same State claiming Lands under Grants of different States, and between a State, or the Citizens thereof, and foreign States, Citizens or Subjects.

In all Cases affecting Ambassadors, other public Ministers and Consuls, and those in which a State shall be a Party, the supreme Court shall have original Jurisdiction. In all the other Cases before mentioned, the Supreme Court shall have appellate Jurisdiction, both as to Law and Fact, with such Exceptions, and under such Regulations as the Congress shall make.

The Trial of all Crimes, except in Cases of Impeachment, shall be by Jury; and such Trial shall be held in the State where the said Crimes shall have been committed; but when not committed within any State, the Trial shall be at such Place or Places as the Congress may by Law have directed.

SECTION 3

Treason against the United States, shall consist only in levying War against them, or in adhering to their Enemies, giving them Aid and Comfort. No Person shall be convicted of Treason unless on the testimony of two Witnesses to the same overt Act, or on Confession in open court.

The Congress shall have Power to declare the Punishment of Treason, but no Attainder of Treason shall work Corruption of Blood, or Forfeiture except during the Life of the Person attainted.

ARTICLE IV

SECTION 1
Full Faith and Credit shall be given in each State to the public Acts, Records, and judicial Proceedings of every other State. And the Congress may by general Laws prescribe the Manner in which such Acts, Records and Proceedings shall be proved, and the Effect thereof.

SECTION 2
The Citizens of each State shall be entitled to all Privileges and Immunities of Citizens in the several States.

A Person charged in any State with Treason, Felony, or other Crime, who shall flee from Justice, and be found in another State, shall on Demand of the executive Authority of the State from which he fled, be delivered up, to be removed to the State having Jurisdiction of the Crime.

No Person held to Service or Labour in one State, under the Laws thereof, escaping into another, shall, in Consequence of any Law or Regulation therein, be discharged from such Service or Labour, but shall be delivered up on Claim of the Party to whom such Service or Labour may be due.

SECTION 3

New States may be admitted by the Congress into this Union; but no new State shall be formed or erected within the Jurisdiction of any other State; nor any State be formed by the Junction of two or more States, or Parts of States, without the Consent of the Legislatures of the States concerned as well as of the Congress.

The Congress shall have Power to dispose of and make all needful Rules and Regulations respecting the Territory or other Property belonging to the United States; and nothing in this Constitution shall be so construed as to Prejudice any Claims of the United States, or of any particular State.

SECTION 4

The United States shall guarantee to every State in this Union a Republican Form of Government, and shall protect each of them against Invasion; and on Application of the Legislature, or of the Executive (when the Legislature cannot be convened) against domestic Violence.

ARTICLE V

The Congress, whenever two thirds of both Houses shall deem it necessary, shall propose Amendments to this Constitution, or, on the Application of the Legislatures of two thirds of the several States, shall call a Convention for proposing Amendments, which, in either Case, shall be valid to all Intents and Purposes, as Part of this Constitution, when ratified by the Legislatures of three fourths of the several States, or by Conventions in three fourths thereof, as the one or the other Mode of Ratification may be proposed by the Congress; Provided that no Amendment which may be made prior to the Year One thousand eight hundred and eight shall in any Manner affect the first and fourth Clauses in the Ninth Section of the first Article; and that no State, without its Consent, shall be deprived of its equal Suffrage in the Senate.

ARTICLE VI

All Debts contracted and Engagements entered into, before the Adoption of this Constitution, shall be as valid against the United States under this Constitution, as under the Confederation.

This Constitution, and the Laws of the United States which shall be made in Pursuance thereof; and all Treaties made, or which shall be made, under the Authority of the United States, shall be the supreme Law of the Land; and the Judges in every State shall be bound thereby, any Thing in the Constitution or Laws of any State to the Contrary notwithstanding.

The Senators and Representatives before mentioned, and the Members of the several State Legislatures, and all executive and judicial Officers, both of the United States and of the several States, shall be bound by Oath or Affirmation, to support this Constitution; but no religious Test shall ever be required as a Qualification to any Office or public Trust under the United States.

ARTICLE VII

The Ratification of the Conventions of nine States, shall be sufficient for the Establishment of this Constitution between the States so ratifying the Same.

FIRST AMENDMENT

Congress shall make no law respecting an establishment of religion, or prohibiting the free exercise thereof; or abridging the freedom of speech, or of the press; or the right of the people peaceably to assemble, and to petition the Government for a redress of grievances.

SECOND AMENDMENT

A well regulated Militia, being necessary to the security of a free State, the right of the people to keep and bear Arms, shall not be infringed.

THIRD AMENDMENT

No Soldier shall, in time of peace be quartered in any house, without the consent of the Owner, nor in time of war, but in a manner to be prescribed by law.

FOURTH AMENDMENT

The right of the people to be secure in their persons, houses, papers, and effects, against unreasonable searches and seizures, shall not be violated, and no Warrants shall issue, but upon probable cause, supported by Oath or affirmation, and particularly describing the place to be searched, and the persons or things to be seized

FIFTH AMENDMENT

No person shall be held to answer for a capital, or otherwise infamous crime, unless on a presentment or indictment of a Grand Jury, except in cases arising in the land or naval forces, or in the Militia, when in actual service in time of War or public danger; nor shall any person be subject for the same offense to be twice put in jeopardy of life or limb; nor shall be compelled in any criminal case to be a witness against himself, nor be deprived of life, liberty, or property, without due process of law; nor shall private property be taken for public use, without just compensation.

SIXTH AMENDMENT

In all criminal prosecutions, the accused shall enjoy the right to a speedy and public trial, by an impartial jury of the State and district wherein the crime shall have been committed, which district shall have been previously ascertained by law, and to be informed of the nature and cause of the accusation; to be confronted with the witnesses against him; to have compulsory process for obtaining witnesses in his favor, and to have the Assistance of Counsel for his defense.

SEVENTH AMENDMENT

In Suits at common law, where the va ue in controversy shall exceed twenty dollars, the r ght of trial by jury shall be preserved, and no fact tried by a jury, shall be otherwise re-examined in any Court of the United States, than according to the rules of the common law.

EIGHTH AMENDMENT

Excessive bail shall not be required, nor excessive fines imposed, nor cruel and unusual punishments inflicted.

NINTH AMENDMENT

The enumeration in the Constitution, of certain rights, shall not be construed to deny or disparage others retained by the people.

TENTH AMENDMENT

The powers not delegated to the United States by the Constitution, nor prohibited by it to the States, are reserved to the States respectively, or to the people.

ELEVENTH AMENDMENT

The Judicial power of the United States shall not be construed to extend to any suit in law or equity, commenced or prosecuted against one of the United States by Citizens of another State, or by Citizens or Subjects of any Foreign State.

TWELFTH AMENDMENT

The Electors shall meet in their respective states, and vote by ballot for President and Vice-President, one of whom, at least, shall not be an inhabitant of the same state with themselves; they shall name in their ballots the person voted for as President, and in distinct ballots the person voted for as Vice-President, and they shall make distinct lists of all persons voted for as President, and of all persons voted for as Vice-President, and of the number of votes for each, which lists they shall sign and certify, and transmit sealed to the seat of the government of the United States, directed to the President of the Senate;–The President of the Senate shall, in the presence of the Senate and House of Representatives, open all the certificates and the votes shall then be counted;–The person having the greatest number of votes for President, shall be the President, if such number be a majority of the whole number of Electors appointed; and if no person have such majority, then from the persons having the highest numbers not exceeding three on the list of those voted for as President, the House of Representatives shall choose immediately, by ballot, the President. But in choosing the President, the votes shall be taken by states, the representation from each state having one vote; a quorum for this purpose shall consist of a member or members from two-thirds of the states, and a majority of all the states shall be necessary to a choice. [And if the House of Representatives shall not choose a President whenever the right of choice shall devolve upon them, before the fourth day of March next following, then the Vice-President shall act as President, as in the case of the death or other constitutional disability of the President.–]The person having the greatest number of votes as Vice-President, shall be the Vice-President, if such number be a majority of the whole number of Electors appointed, and if no person have a majority, then from the two highest numbers on the list, the Senate shall choose the Vice-President; a quorum for the purpose shall consist of two-thirds of the whole number of Senators, and a majority of the whole number shall be necessary to a choice. But no person constitutionally ineligible to the office of President shall be eligible to that of Vice-President of the United States.

THIRTEENTH AMENDMENT

SECTION 1
Neither slavery nor involuntary servitude, except as a punishment for crime whereof the party shall have been duly convicted, shall exist within the United States, or any place subject to their jurisdiction.

SECTION 2
Congress shall have power to enforce this article by appropriate legislation.

FOURTEENTH AMENDMENT

SECTION 1
All persons born or naturalized in the United States, and subject to the jurisdiction thereof, are citizens of the United States and of the State wherein they reside. No State shall make or enforce any law which shall abridge the privileges or immunities of citizens of the United States; nor shall any State deprive any person of life, liberty, or property, without due process of law; nor deny to any person within its jurisdiction the equal protection of the laws.

SECTION 2
Representatives shall be apportioned among the several States according to their respective numbers, counting the whole number of persons in each State, excluding Indians not taxed. But when the right to vote at any election for the choice of

electors for President and Vice-President of the United States, Representatives in Congress, the Executive and Judicial officers of a State, or the members of the Legislature thereof, is denied to any of the male inhabitants of such State, being twenty-one years of age, and citizens of the United States, or in any way abridged, except for participation in rebellion, or other crime, the basis of representation therein shall be reduced in the proportion which the number of such male citizens shall bear to the whole number of male citizens twenty-one years of age in such State.

SECTION 3

No Person shall be a Senator or Representative in Congress, or elector of President and Vice-President, or hold any office, civil or military, under the United States, or under any State, who, having previously taken an oath, as a member of Congress, or as an officer of the United States, or as a member of any State legislature, or as an executive or judicial officer of any State, to support the Constitution of the United States, shall have engaged in insurrection or rebellion against the same, or given aid or comfort to the enemies thereof. But Congress may by a vote of two-thirds of each House, remove such disability.

SECTION 4

The validity of the public debt of the United States, authorized by law, including debts incurred for payment of pensions and bounties for services in suppressing insurrection or rebellion, shall not be questioned. But neither the United States nor any State shall assume or pay any debt or obligation incurred in aid of insurrection or rebellion against the United States, or any claim for the loss or emancipation of any slave; but all such debts, obligations and claims shall be held illegal and void.

SECTION 5

The Congress shall have the power to enforce, by appropriate legislation, the provisions of this article.

FIFTEENTH AMENDMENT

SECTION 1

The right of citizens of the United States to vote shall not be denied or abridged by the United States or by any State on account of race, color, or previous condition of servitude–

SECTION 2

The Congress shall have the power to enforce this article by appropriate legislation.

SIXTEENTH AMENDMENT

The Congress shall have power to lay and collect taxes on incomes, from whatever source derived, without apportionment among the several States, and without regard to any census or enumeration.

SEVENTEENTH AMENDMENT

The Senate of the United States shall be composed of two Senators from each State, elected by the people thereof, for six years; and each Senator shall have one vote. The electors in each State shall have the qualifications requisite for electors of the most numerous branch of the State legislatures.

When vacancies happen in the representation of any State in the Senate, the executive authority of such State shall issue writs of election to fill such vacancies: Provided, That the legislature of any State may empower the executive thereof to make temporary appointments until the people fill the vacancies by election as the legislature may direct.

This amendment shall not be so construed as to affect the election or term of any Senator chosen before it becomes valid as part of the Constitution.

EIGHTEENTH AMENDMENT

SECTION 1
After one year from the ratification of this article the manufacture, sale, or transportation of intoxicating liquors within, the importation thereof into, or the exportation thereof from the United States and all territory subject to the jurisdiction thereof for beverage purposes is hereby prohibited.

SECTION 2
The Congress and the several States shall have concurrent power to enforce this article by appropriate legislation.

SECTION 3
This article shall be inoperative unless it shall have been ratified as an amendment to the Constitution by the legislatures of the several States, as provided in the Constitution, within seven years from the date of the submission hereof to the States by the Congress.

NINETEENTH AMENDMENT

SECTION 1
The right of citizens of the United States to vote shall not be denied or abridged by the United States or by any State on account of sex.

SECTION 2
Congress shall have power to enforce this article by appropriate legislation.

TWENTIETH AMENDMENT

SECTION 1
The terms of the President and Vice President shall end at noon on the 20th day of January, and the terms of Senators and Representatives at noon on the 3d day of January, of the years in which such terms would have ended if this article had not been ratified; and the terms of their successors shall then begin.

SECTION 2
The Congress shall assemble at least once in every year, and such meeting shall begin at noon on the 3d day of January, unless they shall by law appoint a different day.

SECTION 3
If, at the time fixed for the beginning of the term of the President, the President elect shall have died, the Vice President elect shall become President. If a President shall not have been chosen before the time fixed for the beginning of his term, or if the President elect shall have failed to qualify, then the

Vice President elect shall act as President until a President shall have qualified; and the Congress may by law provide for the case wherein neither a President elect nor a Vice President elect shall have qualified, declaring who shall then act as President, or the manner in which one who is to act shall be selected, and such person shall act accordingly until a President or Vice President shall have qualified.

SECTION 4
The Congress may by law provide for the case of the death of any of the persons from whom the House of Representatives may choose a President whenever the right of choice shall have devolved upon them, and for the case of the death of any of the persons from whom the Senate may choose a Vice President whenever the right of choice shall have devolved upon them.

SECTION 5
Sections 1 and 2 shall take effect on the 15th day of October following the ratification of this article.

SECTION 6
This article shall be inoperative unless it shall have been ratified as an amendment to the Constitution by the legislatures of three-fourths of the several States within seven years from the date of its submission.

TWENTY-FIRST AMENDMENT

SECTION 1
The eighteenth article of amendment to the Constitution of the United States is hereby repealed.

SECTION 2

The transportation or importation into any State, Territory, or possession of the United States for delivery or use therein of intoxicating liquors, in violation of the laws thereof, is hereby prohibited.

SECTION 3

This article shall be inoperative unless it shall have been ratified as an amendment to the Constitution by conventions in the several States, as provided in the Constitution, within seven years from the date of the submission hereof to the States by the Congress.

TWENTY-SECOND AMENDMENT

SECTION 1

No person shall be elected to the office of the President more than twice, and no person who has held the office of President, or acted as President, for more than two years of a term to which some other person was elected President shall be elected to the office of the President more than once. But this Article shall not apply to any person holding the office of President when this Article was proposed by the Congress, and shall not prevent any person who may be holding the office of President, or acting as President, during the term within which this Article becomes operative from holding the office of President or acting as President during the remainder of such term.

SECTION 2

This Article shall be inoperative unless it shall have been ratified as an amendment to the Constitution by the legislatures of three-fourths of the several

States within seven years from the date of its submission to the States by the Congress.

TWENTY-THIRD AMENDMENT

SECTION 1
The District constituting the seat of Government of the United States shall appoint in such manner as the Congress may direct:

A number of electors of President and Vice President equal to the whole number of Senators and Representatives in Congress to which the District would be entitled if it were a State, but in no event more than the least populous State; they shall be in addition to those appointed by the States, but they shall be considered, for the purposes of the election of President and Vice President, to be electors appointed by a State; and they shall meet in the District and perform such duties as provided by the twelfth article of amendment.

SECTION 2
The Congress shall have power to enforce this article by appropriate legislation.

TWENTY-FOURTH AMENDMENT

SECTION 1
The right of citizens of the United States to vote in any primary or other election for President or Vice President, for electors for President or Vice President, or for Senator or Representative in Congress, shall not be denied or abridged by the

United States or any State by reason of failure to pay any poll tax or other tax.

SECTION 2
The Congress shall have power to enforce this article by appropriate legislation.

TWENTY-FIFTH AMENDMENT

SECTION 1
In case of the removal of the President from office or of his death or resignation, the Vice President shall become President.

SECTION 2
Whenever there is a vacancy in the office of the Vice President, the President shall nominate a Vice President who shall take office upon confirmation by a majority vote of both Houses of Congress.

SECTION 3
Whenever the President transmits to the President *pro tempore* of the Senate and the Speaker of the House of Representatives his written declaration that he is unable to discharge the powers and duties of his office, and until he transmits to them a written declaration to the contrary, such powers and duties shall be discharged by the Vice President as Acting President.

SECTION 4
Whenever the Vice President and a majority of either the principal officers of the executive departments or of such other body as Congress may by law provide, transmit to the President *pro tempore* of the Senate and the Speaker of the House of Representatives

their written declaration that the President is unable to discharge the powers and duties of his office, the Vice President shall immediately assume the powers and duties of the office as Acting President.

Thereafter, when the President transmits to the President *pro tempore* of the Senate and the Speaker of the House of Representatives his written declaration that no inability exists, he shall resume the powers and duties of his office unless the Vice President and a majority of either the principal officers of the executive department or of such other body as Congress may by law provide, transmit within four days to the President *pro tempore* of the Senate and the Speaker of the House of Representatives their written declaration that the President is unable to discharge the powers and duties of his office. Thereupon Congress shall decide the issue, assembling within forty-eight hours for that purpose if not in session. If the Congress within twenty-one days after receipt of the latter written declaration, or, if Congress is not in session, within twenty-one days after Congress is required to assemble, determines by two-thirds vote of both Houses that the President is unable to discharge the powers and duties of his office, the Vice President shall continue to discharge the same as Acting President; otherwise, the President shall resume the powers and duties of his office.

TWENTY-SIXTH AMENDMENT

SECTION 1
The right of citizens of the United States, who are eighteen years of age or older, to vote shall not be denied or abridged by the United States or by any State on account of age.

SECTION 2

The Congress shall have power to enforce this article by appropriate legislation.

TWENTY-SEVENTH AMENDMENT

No law, varying the compensation for the services of the Senators and Representatives, shall take effect, until an election of Representatives shall have intervened.

DECLARATION OF INDEPENDENCE
A TRANSCRIPTION

Note: The following text is a transcription of the Stone Engraving of the parchment Declaration of Independence (the document on display in the Rotunda at the National Archives Museum.) The spelling and punctuation reflects the original.

In Congress, July 4, 1776.
The unanimous Declaration of the thirteen united States of America,

When in the Course of human events, it becomes necessary for one people to dissolve the political bands which have connected them with another, and to assume among the powers of the earth, the separate and equal station to which the Laws of Nature and of Nature's God entitle them, a decent respect to the opinions of mankind requires that they should declare the causes which impel them to the separation.

We hold these truths to be self-evident, that all men are created equal, that they are endowed by their Creator with certain unalienable Rights, that among these are Life, Liberty and the pursuit of Happiness.--That to secure these rights, Governments are instituted among Men, deriving their just powers from the consent of the governed, --That whenever any Form of Government becomes destructive of these ends, it is the Right of the People to alter or to abolish it, and to institute new Government, laying its foundation on such principles and organizing its powers in such form, as to them shall seem most likely to effect their Safety and

Happiness. Prudence, indeed, will dictate that Governments long established should not be changed for light and transient causes; and accordingly all experience hath shewn, that mankind are more disposed to suffer, while evils are sufferable, than to right themselves by abolishing the forms to which they are accustomed. But when a long train of abuses and usurpations, pursuing invariably the same Object evinces a design to reduce them under absolute Despotism, it is their right, it is their duty, to throw off such Government, and to provide new Guards for their future security.-- Such has been the patient sufferance of these Colonies; and such is now the necessity which constrains them to alter their former Systems of Government. The history of the present King of Great Britain is a history of repeated injuries and usurpations, all having in direct object the establishment of an absolute Tyranny over these States. To prove this, let Facts be submitted to a candid world.

He has refused his Assent to Laws, the most wholesome and necessary for the public good.
He has forbidden his Governors to pass Laws of immediate and pressing importance, unless suspended in their operation till his Assent should be obtained; and when so suspended, he has utterly neglected to attend to them.

He has refused to pass other Laws for the accommodation of large districts of people, unless those people would relinquish the right of Representation in the Legislature, a right inestimable to them and formidable to tyrants only.

He has called together legislative bodies at places unusual, uncomfortable, and distant from the depository of their public Records, for the sole purpose of fatiguing them into compliance with his measures.

He has dissolved Representative Houses repeatedly, for opposing with manly firmness his invasions on the rights of the people.

He has refused for a long time, after such dissolutions, to cause others to be elected; whereby the Legislative powers, incapable of Annihilation, have returned to the People at large for their exercise; the State remaining in the mean time exposed to all the dangers of invasion from without, and convulsions within.

He has endeavoured to prevent the population of these States; for that purpose obstructing the Laws for Naturalization of Foreigners; refusing to pass others to encourage their migrations hither, and raising the conditions of new Appropriations of Lands.

He has obstructed the Administration of Justice, by refusing his Assent to Laws for establishing Judiciary powers.

He has made Judges dependent on his Will alone, for the tenure of their offices, and the amount and payment of their salaries.

He has erected a multitude of New Offices, and sent hither swarms of Officers to harrass our people, and eat out their substance.

He has kept among us, in times of peace, Standing Armies without the Consent of our legislatures.

He has affected to render the Military independent of and superior to the Civil power.

He has combined with others to subject us to a jurisdiction foreign to our constitution, and unacknowledged by our laws; giving his Assent to their Acts of pretended Legislation:

For Quartering large bodies of armed troops among us:

For protecting them, by a mock Trial, from punishment for any Murders which they should commit on the Inhabitants of these States:

For cutting off our Trade with all parts of the world:

For imposing Taxes on us without our Consent:

For depriving us in many cases, of the benefits of Trial by Jury:

For transporting us beyond Seas to be tried for pretended offences

For abolishing the free System of English Laws in a neighbouring Province, establishing therein an Arbitrary government, and enlarging its Boundaries so as to render it at once an example and fit instrument for introducing the same absolute rule into these Colonies:

For taking away our Charters, abolishing our most valuable Laws, and altering fundamentally the Forms of our Governments:

For suspending our own Legislatures, and declaring themselves invested with power to legislate for us in all cases whatsoever.

He has abdicated Government here, by declaring us out of his Protection and waging War against us.

He has plundered our seas, ravaged our Coasts, burnt our towns, and destroyed the lives of our people.

He is at this time transporting large Armies of foreign Mercenaries to compleat the works of death, desolation and tyranny, already begun with circumstances of Cruelty & perfidy scarcely paralleled in the most barbarous ages, and totally unworthy the Head of a civilized nation.

He has constrained our fellow Citizens taken Captive on the high Seas to bear Arms against their Country, to become the executioners of their friends and Brethren, or to fall themselves by their Hands.

He has excited domestic insurrections amongst us, and has endeavoured to bring on the inhabitants of our frontiers, the merciless Indian Savages, whose known rule of warfare, is an undistinguished destruction of all ages, sexes and conditions.

In every stage of these Oppressions We have Petitioned for Redress in the most humble terms: Our repeated Petitions have been answered only by repeated injury. A Prince whose character is thus marked by every act which may define a Tyrant, is unfit to be the ruler of a free people.

Nor have We been wanting in attentions to our British brethren. We have warned them from time to time of attempts by their legislature to extend an unwarrantable jurisdiction over us. We have reminded them of the circumstances of our emigration and settlement here. We have appealed to their native justice and magnanimity, and we have conjured them by the ties of our common kincred to disavow these usurpations, which, would inevitably interrupt our connections and correspondence. They too have been deaf to the voice of justice and of consanguinity. We must, therefore, acquiesce in the necessity, which denounces our Separation, and hold them, as we hold the rest of mankind, Enemies in War, in Peace Friends.

We, therefore, the Representatives of the united States of America, in General Congress, Assembled, appealing to the Supreme Judge of the world for the rectitude of our intentions, do, in the Name, and by Authority of the good People of these Co onies, solemnly publish and declare, That these Jnited Colonies are, and of Right ought to be Free and Independent States; that they are Absolved from all Allegiance to the British Crown, and that all political connection between them and the State of Great Britain, is and ought to be totally dissolved; and that as Free and Independent States, they have full Power to levy War, conclude Peace, ccntract Alliances, establish Commerce, and to do all other Acts and Things which Independent States may of right do. And for the support of this Declaration, with a firm reliance on the protection of divine Providence, we mutually pledge to each other our Lives, our Fortunes and our sacred Honor.

Georgia
Button Gwinnett
Lyman Hall
George Walton

North Carolina
William Hooper
Joseph Hewes
John Penn

South Carolina
Edward Rutledge
Thomas Heyward, Jr.
Thomas Lynch, Jr.
Arthur Middleton

Massachusetts
John Hancock
Maryland
Samuel Chase
William Paca
Thomas Stone
Charles Carroll of Carrollton

Virginia
George Wythe
Richard Henry Lee
Thomas Jefferson
Benjamin Harrison
Thomas Nelson, Jr.
Francis Lightfoot Lee
Carter Braxton

Pennsylvania
Robert Morris
Benjamin Rush
Benjamin Franklin
John Morton
George Clymer
James Smith
George Taylor
James Wilson
George Ross
Delaware
Caesar Rodney
George Read
Thomas McKean

New York
William Floyd
Philip Livingston
Francis Lewis
Lewis Morris

New Jersey
Richard Stockton
John Witherspoon
Francis Hopkinson
John Hart
Abraham Clark

New Hampshire
Josiah Bartlett
William Whipple

Massachusetts
Samuel Adams
John Adams
Robert Treat Paine
Elbridge Gerry

Rhode Island
Stephen Hopkins
William Ellery

Connecticut
Roger Sherman
Samuel Huntington
William Williams
Oliver Wolcott

New Hampshire
Matthew Thornton

Governmental System in the Commonwealth of Pennsylvania

There are three co-equal branches of government: Executive, Legislative and Judicial

The **Executive branch**
- Led by the Governor and Lieutenant Governor.
- Other offices include the Attorney General, Auditor General, Treasurer various Secretarial positions (i.e. Secretary of Agriculture, etc) and Commissions.

The **Legislative branch** consists of the General Assembly, including House and Senate. The population of the Commonwealth is divided in "districts" for both the House and Senate. General Assembly and Federal districts are re-drawn by the Legislature every 10 years, following the completion of the Federal Census. Once the maps are passed by both Houses, the Governor must also approve them before they can be used.

The Senate
- Led by the Lieutenant Governor when present or by the President *pro tempore* (*pro tempore* is Latin for "temporarily" or "for the time being").
- The President *pro tempore* is selected from the majority party. The majority party senators serve in this position on a rotating basis.
- There are currently 50 Senators and their term is 4 years.
- Every 2 years 25 Senators are elected, the other 25 are elected 2 years later.

<u>The House of Representatives</u>
- Led by the Speaker of the House. The Speaker is elected by the majority party.
- There are currently 203 representatives and they serve for a term of 2 years.
- All members of the House are up for re-election every 2 years.

The **Judicial branch** is led by the Supreme Court of Pennsylvania.

<u>State Supreme Court</u>
- Has 9 judges who are elected and may serve until they are 75 years old.
- Judges are nominated for retention (to keep their job) every 10 years.

<u>Other courts in Pennsylvania:</u>
- Courts of Common Pleas
- Superior Court
- Commonwealth Court
- Minor courts, include Magisterial District Judges, Municipal Court Judges.

For more information on the court system, please visit: http://www.pacourts.us/learn

Pennsylvania Flag

Coat of Arms

The Pennsylvania coat of arms is on the flag.
It was designed by Caleb Lownes in 1778 and was
officially adopted in 1907.

Elements of the Coat of Arms:
- Shield—emblazoned with three symbols of the
  Commonwealth:
    - Ship—representing commerce
    - Clay red plow—representing natural resources
    - Three sheaves of wheat—representing
      agriculture, wealth of thought and wealth of
      action
- American Bald Eagle—representing Pennsylvania's
  loyalty to the nation
- Draft Horses—representing the working support of
  agriculture and commerce
- Olive branch—symbol of peace
- Cornstalk—symbol of prosperity
- State motto: virtue, liberty and independence

William Penn

The life of William Penn is full of interesting events and people. Like a tapestry, threads were woven together, to create a man uniquely positioned to influence world events. Just like us, Penn couldn't see the final tapestry he was a part of while he was living it. He would never get to see the full impact his simple faith and daring nature had on the country that was to become the United States of America. Even after over 250 years, that story is still being written. May Penn's life be an inspiration to all who learn about this man of faith and action.

1644 - Born in London. His parents were Sir William and Margaret Penn. Penn's father was an admiral in the English Navy.

1649 - Charles I is beheaded.

1656 - Admiral William Penn is stripped of his command. He moves his family, including young William to Macroom Castle in Ireland. While there, William becomes familiar with nature and learns skills that will be used when moving to Pennsylvania.

1658 - Cromwell dies. Admiral Penn is appointed to Parliament.

1660 - begins attendance at Oxford University. Compulsory membership to the Church of England frustrates Penn. The roots of religious freedom are planted.

1661 - Charles II becomes King of England.

1662 - Penn leaves Oxford to study abroad in France

1665 - Enters law school. He leaves shortly after and joins the navy. He then is called home to manage the family estate in Ireland.

1667 - Becomes a Quaker after hearing Thomas Loe speak.

1670 - Penn's father dies, leaving him with money and property. Amongst his wealth, is an iou from King Charles II equivalent to 16,000 pounds (approximately $3.7 million today)

1672 - Marries Gulielma Springett

1681 - Penn is granted land, which will become Pennsylvania, by King Charles II.

1682 - Penn arrives in Pennsylvania and writes the Frame of Government. He negotiates the Great Treaty of Shackamaxon. Penn purchases land from the Lenni Lenape (Delaware Indians). The treaty becomes the only treaty not broken by European settlers in the United States. Establishes the capital city of Philadelphia.

1684 - Returns to England to see the king, the goal: to settle a land dispute with Charles Calvert, third Lord of Baltimore.

1685 - James II becomes king. James and Penn were childhood friends.

1687 - James frees religious prisoners

1688 - James was removed from the throne and replaced by William III & Mary II. Pennsylvania Quakers lead the protests against slavery.

1689 - Penn was sent to the Tower of London for treason. He is released after two weeks and loses the Pennsylvania Colony. Three years pass before Penn is cleared of the charge of treason.

1694 - Gulielma dies. King William returns Penn's land.

1696 - Penn marries Hannah Callowhill.

1699 - Returns to America. His goal: to establish a plan that would allow the colonies to work together and prevent the king from taking control of the colony again.

1701 - returns to England to present his plan to the king. He is successful in convincing the king to allow him to retain control of the colony.

1708 - Penn is sued for money owed to an associate. He could not pay the debt and was imprisoned in the Tower of London. In time, he is released, but is plagued by health issues.

1712 - Suffers several strokes, affecting his speech and memory.

1718 - Dies in Ruscombe, England

Quick Facts

Founded: 1691

Founder: William Penn

State Capital: Harrisburg

Number of Counties: 67

State Constitution: adopted in 1691

State Motto: *Virtue, Liberty and Independence*

State Song: "Pennsylvania" by Eddie Khoury
and Ronnie Bonner

State Animal: White-tailed deer

State Amphibian: Eastern Hellbender

State Bird: Ruffed grouse

State Dog: Great Dane

State Fish: Brook trout

State Flower: Mountain laurel

State Fossil: Trilobite

State Insect: Firefly

State Plant: Penngift crownvetch

State Tree: Eastern hemlock

State Aircraft: Piper J-3 Cub

State Arboretum: Morris Arboretum & Gardens

State Beverage: Milk

State Firearm: Pennsylvania Long Rifle

State Flagship: U.S. Brig Niagara

State Locomotive 1: K4s Steam Locomotive

State Locomotive 2: GGI 4859 Electric Locomotive

State Nickname: The Keystone State

State Pops Orchestra: Philly POPS

Coat of Arms: adopted 1778

State Flag: First authorized in 1799. In 1907 the blue field of the flag was standardized to match the United States flag by the General Assembly.

State Colors: Blue and Gold

Major Rivers: Allegheny, Delaware, Lehigh, Monongahela, Ohio, Schuylkill, Susquehanna

Pennsylvania is considered a Commonwealth, not a state. In a Commonwealth, the ultimate power lies with the people, not the state.

Pennsylvania
by
Eddie Khoury & Ronnie Bonner

Pennsylvania, Pennsylvania,
Mighty is your name,
Steeped in glory and tradition,
Object of acclaim.
Where brave men fought the foe of freedom,
Tyranny decried,
'Til the bell of independence
filled the countryside.

CHORUS

Pennsylvania, Pennsylvania,
May your future be,
filled with honor everlasting
as your history.

VERSE 2

Pennsylvania, Pennsylvania,
Blessed by God's own hand,
Birthplace of a mighty nation,
Keystone of the land.
Where first our country's flag unfolded,
Freedom to proclaim,
May the voices of tomorrow
glorify your name.

Why is Pennsylvania called the "Keystone State?"

A keystone is the wedge shaped middle stone in an arch. Its main job is to strengthen the arch, while holding the rest of the stones in place. The keystone is the "glue" that holds everything together.

After the American Revolution, Pennsylvania became known as "The Keystone State" because of its strategic role in holding the fledgling United States together. It was the epicenter of political, economic, artistic, medical, military and agricultural advancements. Philadelphia, the new nations first capital, was home to many notable "firsts". It was the location of the first museum, medical college for women, college of pharmacy and public schools, just to name a few. It still boasts some of our country's most influential historic landmarks. From Constitution Hall to the Liberty Bell in Philadelphia, Gettysburg and other notable locations throughout the Commonwealth, the history of our nation runs deep and true.

Pennsylvania was uniquely positioned, because of its location geographically, as well as its natural and cultural resources, to be the critical player in the fight for independence. After independence was achieved, Pennsylvania began to lead the new nation forward with the same tenacity it exhibited during the Revolution.

BIBLIOGRAPHY

Baczynski, Bernadette, L. *William Penn: Founder of the Pennsylvania Colony*. Mankato, MN. Capstone Press, 2004.

Cornell, William A. and Millard Altland. *Our Pennsylvania Heritage*. 13th Edition, Penns Valley Publishers. 2003

The Declaration of Independence: https://www.archives.gov/founding-docs/declaration-transcript

Fifty States: https://www.50states.com

Lutz, Norma Jean. *William Penn*. Avondale, PA. Chelsea House Publishers, 2000.

Office of the Chief Clerk, Pennsylvania House of Representatives. *Constitution of the Commonwealth of Pennsylvania*. 2005.

Pennsylvania: http://www.portal.state.pa.us/portal/server.pt/community/things/4280/symbols_of_pennsylvania/478690.

Pennsylvania Constitution (including previous versions): https://www.duq.edu/academics/gumberg-library/pa-constitution

The Pennsylvania Court System: https://system.uslegal.com/state-courts/pennsylvania-state-court/

Pellow, Randall A. & Gary P. Bukoski. Pennsylvania Pride. Third Edition. Landsdale, PA. Penns Valley Publishers, 2004.

The Pennsylvania State Legislature Constitution: https://www.legis.state.pa.us/cfdocs/legis/li/constitution.cfm

Senate of Pennsylvania. Constitution of the Commonwealth of Pennsylvania. 2012

Sommerville, Barbara A. William Penn: Founder of Pennsylvania. Minneapolis, MN. Compass Point Books, 2006.

State Symbols USA: https://statesymbolsusa.org/states/united-states/pennsylvania, accessed 12/1/2019.

The Unified Judicial Court System of Pennsylvania: http://www.pacourts.us/learn

The United States Constitution: https://constitution.congress.gov/constitution/

ACKNOWLEDGEMENTS

Words to express my thanks and gratitude to my husband, Steve, seem inadequate, but I will give it a try. Through the good and bad, he has been a steady rock and encouragement. Without his support, this project would not have gotten off the ground, let alone come to completion.

To my sons, Zachary, Isaac, Josiah and daughter-in-law Sequoyah, who sacrificed time together to allow me to focus on finishing this project. May you read this book and fully comprehend the gift you have been given: the ability to live in freedom. My prayer is you use your God given gifts and freedoms to protect and defend them.

To my friends and fellow writers at Scribe's Oasis: Mandy, Susan, Kelly, Laura, and Julie. You all have been there to give me a "kick in the pants" when I needed it, as well as much love and support. You all have made me a better writer, but most importantly a better person. Thank you.

To my parents, Edward and Gloria who taught me my first lessons of love, hard work, patriotism and sacrifice. You both have shown me what can be accomplished through hard work and determination.

To my sister, Amy and her partner, Kelly. Your love and support mean the world to me and, even though we don't always agree, my love for you is unwavering.

To my mother-in-law Elaine, you have helped me to see the beauty in the world around us through your love of nature and I am so glad we have gotten to know each other better over the last few years.

To Bill, Debbie, Stephanie and Justin. I am so happy to have you all in my life. Thank you for your prayers, support and encouragement.

To my extended family, who is scattered across this great nation, and too numerous to list individually. Though we may be separated by miles, our bonds have helped to shape me into who I am today and I am forever grateful.

This book is also written for William Penn. His sacrifice helped birth a unique commonwealth and ultimately, a nation. A commonwealth founded on religious freedom and a nation, where freedoms granted by our Creator, are recognized. Those most sacred rights are under increasing threat. May we never become so distracted as to neglect the responsibility of protecting our Rights granted by Almighty God or so complacent as to believe man would not try to take them away because of our ignorance to their source.

To those who came before me seeking religious freedom, opportunity and a new life. I pray I willl always be mindful of the gift I have been given and to do everything in my power to pass it on as the legacy they fought so hard to establish. They worked and sacrificed so that future generations might be able to live in peace and prosperity. To them, our humble respect and admiration is due.